YOU CAN UNDERSTAND THE OLD TESTAMENT

You Can Understand the Old Testament

A Book-by-Book Guide for Catholics

Peter Kreeft

CHARIS

Servant Publications
Ann Arbor, Michigan

The chapters in this book first appeared in article form in issues of
the *National Catholic Register* during the years of 1989 and 1990.

Published by Servant Publications
P.O. Box 8617
Ann Arbor, Michigan 48107

Cover design by Michael Andaloro

98 99 10 9 8 7 6 5

Printed in the United States of America
ISBN 0-89283-689-X

Library of Congress Cataloging-in-Publication Data

Kreeft, Peter.
    You can understand the Old Testament / by Peter Kreeft.
        p.   cm.
    ISBN 0-89283-689-X
    1. Bible. O.T.—Textbooks.   I. Title.
BS1194.S42   1991
221.6'1—dc20   90-48287

Contents

AUTHOR'S NOTE

UNLESS OTHERWISE INDICATED, I quote from the Revised Standard Version (RSV) of the Bible. I have chosen this particular version of Scripture because it is both literal and literary, both accurate and beautiful.

Further, I am not a biblical scholar and this is not an authoritative and exhaustive introduction to the Old Testament. It is a popular overview, intended to pique the reader's interest in reading and studying Scripture as God's Word. It is a book for amateurs like myself who want to make a start in understanding the Old Testament. For a more substantial introduction to the Old Testament, the reader should look elsewhere.

General Introduction to the Bible

"YOU CATHOLICS DON'T KNOW THE BIBLE because your church has discouraged Bible reading, because it fears that if you read the Bible the same thing will happen to you as happened to Luther: you'll become Protestants."

The charge is fundamentally false, of course, but we must refute it by actually reading and knowing the Bible, as the Second Vatican Council so strongly encouraged. It is our book, after all. Only the first part of the Protestant charge is true, but it *is* true: most Catholics don't know or read the Bible. It's high time for every single reader of these words to decide to set aside fifteen minutes each day to listen to God. Both prayer and Bible reading are (or should be) listening to God; indeed, the two should blend into each other. We should pray biblically and read prayerfully. I challenge you to give a good excuse—to God, not to me or even to yourself—for not doing that right now.

This book and the one that will follow on the New Testament are designed as practical aids to Catholic Bible reading—which, next to the Mass and prayer, is our most perfect and most important religious activity.

SOME ESSENTIAL POINTS ABOUT THE BIBLE

Where do we begin? First, we mustn't lose the forest for the trees. As we explore the separate trees of the forest (books of the Bible), we must keep in mind what kind of forest (book) it is. Here are some essential things about the whole.

What is the Bible? The word means "book," but it is not one book but many different books from many different authors, times, styles, and literary forms: history, poetry, drama, philosophy, letters, visions, practical advice, songs, prophecy, law, and much more. This is not a book, this is a library. More, this is a world.

Yet there is a unity in all this diversity. Most basically, the Bible is a story. Unlike the holy books of other religions, the Bible tells about real events that happened in history. It is a story of people. As G.K. Chesterton said, "There are only two things that do not get boring: a person and a story, and even a story must be about a person." The persons involved here include the three most important persons of all: the Father, the Son, and the Holy Spirit. The Bible is "stories of God." But it is stories also about us, about our relationships with each other and with God. The horizontal (people to people) and vertical (people to God) relationships meet here and form a cross.

But what kind of story is this? Is it a war story or a detective story or a love story or what? It matters because we are still in this story, still part of this story. Does the Bible tells us what kind of a story we are in, what our life is all about?

Yes. It is a love story because "God is love." That is his plan and point and purpose in all that he does. The Bible is the great love story between God and "the people of God."

The story unfolds in three acts. Theologians call them creation, fall, and redemption. They fit the three stages of every story ever told: first, a situation is set up; then it is somehow upset by a problem or conflict or challenge; finally, it is reset, successfully or unsuccessfully. Paradise, Paradise Lost, and Paradise Regained are the three stages here, and the third stage begins as early as the third chapter of Genesis, when God begins to redeem, or buy back, fallen mankind. This third act has three sub-scenes. First, God reveals himself as a Father, in the Old Testament; then, as Jesus the Son in the Gospels; finally, as the Holy Spirit in Acts and all of the time that follows, the age of Christ's church on earth. That is the part of the story we are in.

The books of the Bible in both testaments are divided into three main categories: history, wisdom, and prophecy. Thus the Bible encompasses past (history), present (wisdom), and future (prophecy). But its history books are more than records of the past; they tell us truths that are just as true of the present. And its wisdom books tell truths that are timeless, not just for the present time. Finally, its prophets do not merely foretell the future, but forth-tell God's truth to all times. The Bible is God's continual prophet telling men and women of every time, and therefore of our time, the truths we need to know for our lives on earth and the way to life in eternity (see John 14:6).

The fundamental choice every reader must make about the Bible is whether or not to believe its claim to be divinely inspired. Is this God's Word about man, or is it man's word about God? Is it God's way down to us, God's revelation? Or is it only man's speculations and gropings up to God? It *claims* to be the first of those two things; if it is not, it cannot give us what it claims to give: four things we need most, four things God has, four things that are gifts from God.

ARE THE CLAIMS OF THE BIBLE TRUE?

First, the Bible claims to give truth—the kind of truth that is "tried and true" (see Psalm 12:6), that "stands true" (see Isaiah 40:8), that is "made true" or performed (see Ezekiel 12:25), that "comes true" as the fulfillment of a promise (see Matthew 5:17-18).

Second, it claims to have power. It uses images like fire and a hammer (Jeremiah 23:29) to refer to itself. It calls itself the "sword of the Spirit" (Ephesians 6:17).

Third, it gives life. Its words "bring God's life-giving Spirit" (John 6:63). Jesus also calls it *seed* (Luke 8), a living, growing thing. Hebrews 4:12 says, "For the word of God is living and active, sharper than any two-edged sword, piercing to the division of soul and spirit, . . . discerning the thoughts and intentions of the heart." Physical swords only cut bodies; this cuts souls, opens souls, heals souls. For this sword comes alive in the hands of a divine swordsman, the Holy Spirit. When you read it, beware: it is reading you. It is not safe and passive, like a rock. It is like a rock you sit on and then it moves; it turns out to be an animal. "Look out! It's alive!"

Fourth, the Bible gives joy and delight, for these are the very substance of God, the very life of God. The Psalms are full of expressions of joy in God's Word (e.g., 1:2; 19:8; 119:97, 103). Jeremiah says to God, ". . . thy words became to me a joy" (15:16). For this is not just a book; this is a love letter, written by God Almighty to you, the individual, not "junk mail" addressed to "dear occupant"! God says to each one of us, "I have called you by name, you are mine" (Isaiah 43:1). The words "I love you" are magic words; they change us when we hear them spoken to us. How much more when we hear them from God!

If you let this book speak to you, you will find it shows you both God and yourself. Just as Jesus revealed to each person he met not only himself but also themselves in a new way, so this book reveals both God and ourselves. It is a mirror.

This book is called "the Word of God." But it points beyond itself to the "Word of God," Jesus Christ. We humans can only utter words that are not alive, but God utters a literally living Word, and that is his Son Jesus. Meeting him is the point of the whole Bible (see John 5:39)— in fact, the point of our lives.

Whether you have ever read the Bible or not, it can be

totally new. What happened in Ezekiel's vision, when the dry bones came to life (see Ezekiel 37), can happen to you as you read this book. Read it above all prayerfully; talk to God as you read it; ask him what he wants to show you. Remember this is not a dead book about the past, but a living letter from God to you in this present moment. For as Jesus says, "He is not the God of the dead, but of the living" (Matthew 22:32).

TIPS FOR READING THE BIBLE

Here are some specific suggestions as to how to read the Bible.

1. At first, forget commentaries and books that tell you what the Bible means; read the Bible itself. Get it "straight from the horse's mouth." The Bible is the most interesting book ever written, but some of the books about it are the dullest books ever written.

2. Read repeatedly. You can never exhaust the riches in this book. The greatest theologians, the greatest saints, and the greatest philosophers never exhaust it; neither will you.

3. First read quickly, to get an overall idea of the book or chapter. Then go back and read slowly and carefully. Don't rush. Relish, ponder, meditate, think, question, sink slowly into the verses that seem to invite you to swim in them.

4. Try to read without prejudice. Let the author speak to you. Don't impose your ideas on the author. Listen first before you talk back.

5. Once you've listened, do talk back. Dialog with the author as if he were living and standing in front of you. Ask him questions, and then go to his book to see what he answers. Ask *God* questions. He's a good teacher; he loves his students to ask questions.

6. Don't confuse (a) understanding with (b) evaluating. That is, don't confuse (a) interpreting with (b) criticizing.

First understand, then evaluate. First let the book talk to you, then talk back. This sounds simple, but it's harder to do than you probably think. For instance, many people *interpret* the Bible's miracle stories as myths because they don't *believe* in miracles. That's simply bad *interpretation*. Whether the miracles really happened or not, the first question is: what is the author trying to say? Is he telling a parable, a fable, or a myth? Or is he telling a story that he claims really happened? That is the first question. The second question is whether you agree with him. But don't let the second question come first. Don't say, for instance, "I don't *agree* that Jesus really rose from the dead, therefore I *interpret* the resurrection as a myth." The Gospel writers did not mean to write myth, but fact. If it didn't happen, it is not a myth but a lie.

7. So keep in mind three questions, and ask them in this order: First, what does this passage mean? How do I understand or interpret its meaning? Second, is it true? Do I believe it? Third, so what? What difference does this make to me, to my life? What should I do about it?

8. Look for "the big picture," the main point. Don't lose the forest for the trees. Don't get hung up on a few specific passages or points. Interpret each passage in its context.

9. After you've read a passage, go back and analyze it. Outline it. Get it clear. Don't be satisfied with a vague feeling. Try to find the structures of thought.

10. Be honest—in reading this or any other book, but especially this book, because of its great claims on you. There is only one honest reason for believing the Bible: because it is true. Not because it is comforting or challenging or up-to-date or useful or relevant. If it were all of those things *but not true*, you should *not* believe it, if you are honest. Seek the truth; "seek, and you will find" (Matthew 7:7). That's a promise.

Introduction to the Old Testament

THE FIRST AND LONGEST HALF of the Bible is called by Christians the "Old Testament" (or Covenant or Promise). Jews call it simply their Bible, or sacred Scriptures. They too believe it is divinely inspired, but they do not believe this about the New Testament, unless they are "Messianic (Christian) Jews." Jews worship the same God Christians worship, but not the same Messiah (Christ).

The Old Testament story distinguishes Judaism (and Christianity) from all other religions of the world in two main ways. First, we find here a religion based on historical facts, not just abstract ideas and ideals. Second, the God of the Old Testament differs from the gods of other religions in at least four important ways:

1. Only a few individuals in the ancient world, like Socrates in Greece and Ahkenaton in Egypt, rose above their society's polytheism (belief in many gods) to monotheism (belief in one God), like the Jews.

2. Only the Jews had the knowledge of creation, of a God who created the entire universe out of nothing.

3. Other peoples separated religion and morality. Only the God of the Bible was perfectly good, righteous, and holy, and the giver of the moral law, demanding moral goodness in all men and women.

4. These differences are accounted for by a fourth one: although other peoples sometimes arrive at profound truths about God by their imagination (myth), their reason (philosophy), and their experience (mysticism), they mixed these

truths with falsehoods because they did not have a revelation from God himself. Other religions tell of man's search for God; the Bible tells of God's search for man. Other religions tell timeless truths about God; the Bible tells of God's deeds in time, in history.

God reveals himself both through words (especially the law given to Moses and the words of the prophets, God's mouthpieces) and deeds. These deeds are both supernatural (miracles) and natural (providence, God providing for his people).

Throughout the Old Testament story, God selects his special instruments: Abel (not Cain), Noah (not the rest of the world), Abram (not Lot), Isaac (not Ishmael), Jacob (not Esau), Joseph (not his brothers), and, in general, the Jews (not the Gentiles)—until Christ the Messiah finally comes. Then Christ's church, the New Israel, spreads the knowledge of the true God, the same God of Israel, throughout the world. Jews do not prosyletize. Christians do. But both worship the same God.

Until that time, God's providential care created, preserved, and educated the nation of Israel to be like a womb, like a mother for the coming Messiah. When Jesus was born from Mary's womb, she became the fulfillment of all that Israel was about.

Yet God is not finished with Israel, even now, according to the New Testament (see Romans 10-11). The church as the New Israel does not simply displace the old, any more than a daughter can displace her mother. For the New Testament is not a mere addition to the Old, nor is it the setting aside of the Old. Jesus says in Matthew 5:17, "Think not that I have come to abolish the law and the prophets; I have come not to abolish them but to fulfil them." The Old Testament, like the New, is about Jesus. It is the beginning of the story of salvation, the same story Jesus completes, the same story we are in.

ONE

Begin at the Beginning: Genesis 1-2

W E BEGIN WITH *Genesis* because we want to follow the Red Queen's advice to Alice when she asks how to tell her story: "Begin at the beginning. Then proceed until you come to the end, then stop." The Bible is the only book ever written that has fulfilled that admirably simple instruction to the letter.

"Genesis" means "beginning." The Hebrew title, *Bereshith*, is taken from the first word, "In the beginning." *Genesis* is the book of beginnings—of the universe, of man, of sin, and of salvation (which is the main theme of the whole Bible). Only God has no beginning: "In the beginning, God."

Genesis is the first book of the "Pentateuch," a Greek word meaning "five-volume book" (*Genesis, Exodus, Leviticus, Numgers, and Deuteronomy*). Jews call these five books the "Torah" (law).

According to the earliest Jewish and Christian traditions, Moses wrote *Genesis*. Many modern scholars doubt this, but the Bible contains many references to Moses as an author, though he probably used and edited many older sources.

Like the whole Bible, *Genesis* is history but not scientific history. This does not mean that it is myth or fable, but that its style is often poetic and that its content is selective. The author is like a photographer who points his camera only at the subjects that are important for his purposes, from his point of view. The purpose of the divine author of the Bible, the Holy Spirit, is to tell us about God and his acts of "salvation history."

Thus *Genesis*, like salvation history itself, and in fact like every story, has three parts. First a situation is set up (creation), then upset (fall), then reset (redemption). Generation, degeneration, and regeneration of mankind; Paradise, Paradise Lost, and Paradise Regained.

The action moves from the Garden of Eden to Egypt, from man in innocence and paradise to the chosen people in sin and slavery but hoping for deliverance. The time span of *Genesis* covers more years than all the rest of the Bible together. It is divided into eleven sections, each beginning with "This is the list of the descendants of..." (*elleh toledoth* in Hebrew).

Since the beginning is so crucial and since *Genesis* covers the beginning of all three stages of our story—creation, fall, and redemption—we will take three chapters to explore *Genesis*, one for *Exodus*, and one for the next three books.

THE GOD WHO CREATES OUT OF NOTHING

Genesis begins not just with the beginning of something, but with the beginning of everything. Its first verse uses a word for which there is no equivalent in any other ancient language. The word is *bara'*. It means not just to make but to create, not just to re-form something new out of something old, but to create something wholly new that was simply not there before. Only God can create, for creation in the literal sense (out of nothing) requires infinite power, since there is an infinite gap between nothing and something. Startling as it may seem, no other people ever had creation stories in the true sense of the word, only formation stories. The Jewish notion of creation is an utterly distinctive notion in the history of human thought. When Jewish theologians like Philo and later Christian theologians (who learned it from the Jews) told the Greeks about it, they were ridiculed.

Yet the consequences of this notion of creation are incomparable. They include a radically new notion of God, of nature, and of human beings and human life.

A God who creates out of nothing is radically different from any of the gods of paganism. Having infinite power, he must be one, and not many, not limited by others. Further, to create this entire universe requires not just infinite power but also infinite wisdom (the wisest men on earth have never been able even to make a stable peace or a good society, much less a universe), a fantastic sense of beauty ("poems are made by fools like me, but only God can make a tree"), and infinite generosity (for one who does not even exist cannot possibly deserve to be created).

Without the notion of creation, nature is either denied or worshiped. Ancient Gentiles, lacking the notion of creation, saw nature either as an illusion (in the Orient) or as something sacred (in the West), as the body or local habitation of the gods. Creation frees nature from nothingness and from Godhood.

Further, if God created nature, it is not only real rather than illusory, it is also good rather than evil. *Genesis* repeats the point with liturgical emphasis: at the end of each of his six days of work, God mutters, "Good, good, good." This is why the problem of evil is more crucial for a Jew or a Christian than for anyone else: he is stuck with a theology of delight, and cannot blame evil on the primal glop God was stuck with, since God created the very glop out of which he made the worlds. That's why Genesis 3 has to come after Genesis 1 and 2: to answer the obvious question raised by the creation account. If an all-good God is in charge here, where did evil come from?

Every heresy is based on a truth—a truth taken to extremes and taken away from its living relationship with other truths. The goodness of creation, taken to the extreme of confusing Eden with post-Eden and taken out of its relationship to the fall, becomes the silliness of an overgrown hippie like Matthew Fox or the seriousness of a nature worshiper like his witch friend Starhawk.

The doctine of creation also means that nature is rational. It is not the arbitrary, fallible wills of many gods, or the primal chaos before all gods, but the all-knowing, all-wise will of the one God who designs and controls nature. The doctrine of creation is thus the origin of science. It is no accident that science grew up almost entirely in the West, not in the Orient, where nature was seen as a shifting veil of *maya* (illusion).

Finally, human beings and human lives get a radically new meaning by the doctrine of creation. If God created my very existence, I simply have no being, no essence, and no rights apart from or independent of God. My relationship to God is not an addition, however precious, to my being; it is my very being, my essence. Man is not man and then related to God; to be a human being is to be God's creature, God's servant, God's son or daughter. Not a second of my time, a cent of my money, a drop of my blood or my sweat, or a thought in my head can I truly call my own unless I first call it his. I owe him my all because I owe him my being. The Bible thus does not present a "religion," as a department of life. It presents life itself as essentially, totally, and inescapably religious, that is, God-relational, from its very center.

How did God create? It was strictly a no-sweat operation. He simply spoke his Word. Christ is present in *Genesis*, for Christ is "the Word of God." ". . . all things were made through him, and without him was not anything made that was made" (John 1:3).

THE KEY QUESTION IS "WHY," NOT "HOW"

Did God use evolution? He may have. *Genesis* is not a
science text, so it does not tell us *how* so much as *why*. But
there are hints. Only three times in the creation account is
bara' used: for the creation of matter (1:1), life (1:21), and
humanity (1:27). The other times, God said, "let the waters
bring forth ... ," or "Let the earth bring forth ..." That is, for
most of his acts of creation, he made rather than created. For
example, he used the pre-existing material of "the dust of
the earth for humanity." An ape body? Perhaps. Why not?
Our "image of God" distinctiveness, our personality, is in
the soul, not in our bodies. We are "rational *animals*." God is
not an animal.

In any case, Catholics have seldom had the difficulties and
embarrassments certain Protestants have had about creation versus evolution. Ever since Augustine, they have often
read *Genisis* evolutionarily, and the "days" non-literally.
(The Hebrew word there, *yom*, is usually used non-literally
in Scripture.)

Genesis even goes a long way to resolve the current
feminist furor. On the one hand, it clearly says that "the
image of God" is "male *and* female" (1:27), and that males'
present kind of "rule" over females is a result of the fall
(3:16). On the other hand, it is equally clear that sexual
differentiation is God's natural design, not our artifice.

In fact, God creates everything by differentiating. Form,
species differentiation—this feature of the world is due to
accident, according to materialism; illusion, according to
pantheism; but divine will and design, according to theism.
God is not an egalitarian. Being versus nonbeing, light
versus darkness, the "waters above" (the firmament) versus
the "waters below" (seas, lakes, rivers), seas versus land,
living versus nonliving, plants versus animals, birds versus
fish versus land animals, species versus species, each "after

its kind," animals versus humanity (in God's image)—and Adam versus Eve, man versus woman. Not a sinister trick of nature or society but a wise and benevolent gift of God, maleness and femaleness are causes for rejoicing, not for embarrassment, except to the fallenness that leads us to hide from God and from each other.

No one has ever told this story better. When our first astronaut ventured into space, this was what he read, in awe. It is literally inexhaustible.

Primitive tribes often recite their "creation epics" over the body of a sick or dying person, to bring the person back to the time of beginnings, when God touched time and matter firsthand. Without buying into superstition or magic, I think it is not too much to say that there seems to be such a mysterious power in these words, in these chapters, that something like that practice is to be recommended. Next time you feel like giving God an emergency phone call, try reading Genesis 1. Somehow, it seems to clear away a lot of fog.

TWO

Our Free Fall into Sin: Genesis 3

W E WILL DEVOTE AN ENTIRE CHAPTER to Genesis 3, because the event narrated in these thirty-one verses, the event we call the fall, is one of the three most important events that have ever happened. The other two are the creation and the incarnation. These are the three "big bangs" in our history.

No greater or more far-reaching tragedy has ever happened than this. A nuclear holocaust is a minor inconvenience compared to the primal divorce from the source of all our joy, our goodness, our peace, our wisdom, and our very essence.

If we were to meet unfallen Adam and Eve now (as we may if we visit an unfallen race on another planet), we would either worship them or totally misunderstand and despise them. We would not feel comfortable with them as something like ourselves. The imagination boggles when it tries to conceive the state of original innocence. That is why such a challenging and fascinating theme has hardly ever been tackled by our poets and storytellers, and never with any real success. (Milton's *Paradise Lost* and C.S. Lewis' *Perelandra* come closest.)

WHY THE FALL NEED NOT HAVE HAPPENED

The first lesson obviously taught by the story of the fall is that it was a free fall. It need not have happened. One way of stating this doctrine is C.S. Lewis': if there are other intelligent and free-willed beings on other planets (as seems very likely considering the size of the universe and the divine generosity and imagination), they need not have fallen. To be a person is not necessarily to be a sinful person. To be in God's image is not necessarily to be in a defaced image. To be married to God is not necessarily to have sued for divorce, as we did in this disastrous rebellion.

There are only three basic explanations for evil. It is to be blamed either on God above us, nature below us, or us. Genesis 3 rejects the two convenient excuses that either God or evolution made us this way. The message of Genesis 3 is that the buck stops here. The finger that points blame is curved one hundred eighty degrees.

Jews, who have and believe this Scripture just as Christians do, say they do not believe in "original sin" because they think of that doctrine as Calvinism, as a denial of the goodness of God's creation even when defaced by sin. But Genesis 3 does not teach Calvinistic "total depravity" (except in the sense that we are totally unable to save ourselves without divine grace, which is also taught in Orthodox Judaism). Rather, the forbidden fruit was "the knowledge of *good and evil*," not just evil. There's still a little good in the worst of us, but also a little bad in the best of us.

By the way, the word "knowledge" here means "experience." God wanted to keep us from the knowledge of good-and-evil that comes from experiencing and tasting it (thus the image of the fruit eaten), not from the knowledge that understands it. The same word is used in Genesis 4 for sexual intercourse: Adam "knew" Eve, and the result was not a book but a baby.

WE ARE MORALLY BAD, NOT BAD IN OUR BEING

Genesis 3 does not teach that man is now *ontologically* bad, bad in his *being,* but *morally* bad, bad in his *choices.* God made our being; we make our choices. Yet it is our state of sinfulness, or separation from God (our state of original sin), that leads us to make sinful choices (actual sins). The word "sin" comes from the German *Sunde,* which means "separation." We sin (actual sin) because we are sinners (original sin), just as we sing because we are singers. Sin is not our essence (that remains ontologically good), but it is more than our day-to-day choices; it is our habit, our character. Yet this habit or character in turn was caused by Adam and Eve's first "actual sin" or evil choice, symbolized by the eating of the forbidden fruit.

How are we to blame for what Adam and Eve did? We aren't; we are to blame for what we do. But what we do is conditioned by what they did, just as a baby who is born a drug addict because its mother took drugs during pregnancy, is conditioned by what its mother did. The mystery of heredity is part of the greater mystery of solidarity, of interdependence among individuals, that goes all the way up into the Trinity itself.

The Bible never says we are punished for Adam's sin, but rather that we sinned "in" Adam. There is the mystery of solidarity. Premodern thinkers, less individualistic than we, saw the human race as an organism, like a tree, not an anthill. Each individual (leaf) gets bad sap because the tree as a whole has bad sap. Adam was the acorn, the first bad sap. It's not a matter of imitation, of anthill-like "follow the leader," but of incorporation, just as our salvation through Christ is not a matter of our imitating Christ from without but of being incorporated into Christ from within by faith and baptism. (It's all in Romans 6.)

The account of the fall in Genesis 3, like the account of the creation, is couched in highly poetic, symbolic language. The talking snake and the two trees are, by any intelligent literary standards, meant to be interpreted symbolically, not literally and physically. But what they symbolize is real and literal. The event of the fall must have really happened at some point in real time. For if not, if the fall is merely a timeless truth about our sinfulness projected into the form of a before-and-after story, then there never really was a time of innocence; and in that case, we are sinful not because we freely chose to make ourselves that way, but because God created us that way from the beginning. In that case, God is on the hook and we are off the hook for sin. We are simply his instruments, his smoking gun. If God, not Adam, designed the fall, then God, not Hitler, designed the Holocaust.

FAITH AND WORKS GO TOGETHER
FROM THE BEGINNING

Why did we fall? What could have motivated our first ancestors to exchange the joy of walking with God in the garden of pure paradise for anything else at all? Genesis 3 holds the clue. The first step in the fall was a weakening of faith. St. Paul says, "... whatever does not proceed from faith is sin" (Romans 14:23). The devil's first temptation to Eve was for her to doubt God's word that eating the forbidden fruit meant death (3:2-3). Once Eve let the demonic lever of doubt find a fulcrum in her soul, her will and her acts soon followed. Faith and works from the beginning go together, neither is ever apart from the other. This is why the very first step in the war against sin and for sanctity is to "take every *thought* captive to obey Christ" (2 Corinthians 10:5).

What is the connection between sin and death, its punishment—i.e., between spiritual death of the soul and physical death of the body? It is not an arbitrary one decreed by an angry God, like "I'll smack your hands if you steal

those cookies!'' Rather, it is a natural and inevitable neces-
sity of human nature in its situation of dependence on God
as the source of all life, spiritual and physical. Once this
source of life was gone from the soul by sin (separation), the
necessary consequence was that the body also died. For the
body is one with the soul, not another *thing*. Body and soul
are like the words and the message of a poem, or the color
and the shape of a painting, not like a horse and a cart. Once
the soul freely cut its lifeline to God, the body necessarily
and unfreely fell with it, like two mountaineers bound
together by one rope. Before the fall, our bodies received life
from God, through the obedient soul; thus there was no
reason we should ever die. Now our bodies are dependent
on subsidies from finite nature instead, a source that soon
runs dry.

After the fall, Adam and Eve used the two defense
mechanisms that we've been using ever since: hiding and
passing the blame. First, they hid from God and from each
other, covering themselves, probably their sexual organs,
with clothes. Why their sexual organs? The fall was not a
matter of sex. God had commanded them to "be fruitful and
multiply." Probably because they had hoped, by eating the
forbidden fruit, to fulfill the devil's false promise to be like
God, complete and independent. But their sexual differentiation revealed their incompleteness as individuals and their
dependence on each other.

Their (and our) second escape was to pass the blame.
Adam blamed Eve (v. 12) and Eve blamed the devil (v. 13).
God, of course, accepted (and accepts) neither excuse. The
blame is on us, and God puts it on Christ on the cross.

THE GREAT WAR BEGINS

Christ is present in Genesis 3 as well as in Genesis 1 (as the
creative Word of God). Verse 15 is the Bible's first prophecy
of redemption. It is an outline of all future history. That

history is to be a spiritual war between the children of Eve (ultimately, Christ, the son of the New Eve, Mary) and the children of the devil. Christ shall bruise Satan's head, destroying his power. But Satan shall bruise Christ's heel, on the cross, shall wound God's "Achilles' heel" or weak spot, his assumed humanity.

St. Augustine's masterpiece, *The City of God*, interprets all human history according to Genesis 3:15, as spiritual warfare between "the City of God," God's children through Eve and Mary and Christ, and "the City of the World," Satan's children. Ever since Cain versus Abel, mankind has been at civil war with itself because half of it is still at revolutionary war with God. There are only two kinds of people. We are either God's children or Satan's. Jesus reaffirmed this terrifying truth many times, for example, in John 8:41-47 and in John 3:3.

Genesis 3:15 interprets all human history as a battle. It is neither a mere doom nor a mere blessing. It is neither black nor white, but a checkerboard. Between the old Paradise of Eden lost and the new Paradise of Heaven to be gained, this world must always remain, for all the sons of Adam and daughters of Eve, full of pain in childbirth and thorns and thistles in sweaty work: neither a snake pit nor a hot tub, but a battlefield. This implies a constant call for vigilance, alertness, hope, and fear together. Since we are "east of Eden," our only options are the illusions of a fool's paradise (i.e., modern hedonism and yuppiedom) or the realism of spiritual combat.

God's exile of Adam and Eve from Eden is like death itself: a punishment but a mercy, a "severe mercy." If God had not sent the cherubim (a type of angel) with the flaming sword to bar the gate of Eden, Adam and Eve may have crept back in to eat the fruit of the other tree, the Tree of (Eternal) Life, and established themselves in their sinful nature as eternal. That would have been literally hell on earth, eternal hopelessness.

Death is now God's anesthesia. It is needed to complete his healing operation on us who have contracted the deadly disease of sin. Only in death do we stop wiggling about on the operating table. Then God can penetrate into our deepest heart with his loving but terrifying scalpel.

The perennial temptation is to creep under the angel's flaming sword, to try to create a heaven on earth. The two most popular forms of this are the Oriental form of creating a mystical, inner paradise through yoga and meditation, and the Western form of building a technological heaven on earth. Both are doomed to failure, of course, but the failure is the greatest *not* when it is obvious, and leads to repentance, but when the failure is masked by apparent success. The thorns and thistles are sent to jolt us awake and remind us of our necessities, of where we are, of the battlefield. Since the peace we are seeking comes from God alone, "Woe to those who cry, Peace! Peace! when there is no peace" (Jeremiah 6:14).

THREE

The Divine Rescue Operation: Genesis Continued

T HE THREE STAGES OF HISTORY—creation, fall, and redemption—are reflected in the three parts of *Genesis*. This third chapter explores the third and longest part, God's "redemption" or "buying-back" of his creatures who sold themselves into Satan's slavery.

This began immediately after the fall in chapter three, when God pronounced the "curses" on Satan (vv. 14-15), on Eve (v. 16) and on Adam (vv. 17-19). All these punishments are also mercies for us. These are like tourniquets, stemming the flow of blood, or like quarantines, stopping the spread of disease. The rest of the story of human history is nothing but the working out of these divine measures with men and women, measures which are simultaneously curses and blessings, fears and hopes.

Death is the most obvious example. We know little about many of the names in the genealogies, but we know with certainty the one thing repeated about every single one: "And he died . . . and he died . . . and he died."

The next event narrated, after the fall, is a death—in fact, a murder. Not every death is a murder, but all death is a consequence of sin. Thus murder shows the meaning of death more clearly than a so-called "natural" death does. Cain's murder of Abel is the fall flowing out, like Abel's blood. It is a kind of icon of our whole fratricidal history of violence, both inner and outer, both small and great.

GOD'S RADICAL SURGERY

Such a radical disease requires a radical surgery. The reason God did not accept Cain's bloodless offering of fruit but only Abel's slain sheep is because "without the shedding of blood there is no forgiveness of sins" (Hebrews 9:22; Genesis 4:10).

"The City of God" and "the City of the World" began to exist side by side as opposite movements of the human heart as soon as Adam and Eve fell into "knowing" good and evil rather than good alone. But with Cain and Abel these two "cities" begin to exist as two groups of people. Cain and Abel are the fathers of the two spiritual races that subsequently divide all human history: the damned and the saved, the once-born and the twice-born, flesh and spirit. The difference, though, within the single human species, is far greater than the difference between two different species. The difference between the blessed in heaven and the damned in hell is greater than the difference between cats and dogs.

When we come to Abraham in chapter 12, the style of narrative changes. Historians can pin down specific dates, places, names, and cross-references in secular history from Abraham onward, but there is no way of knowing when Noah lived or perhaps even whether he and his flood are meant to be archetypal symbols or literal facts. Between the symbolic style of the first three chapters and the literal history of the story of the chosen people which begins with the call of Abraham in chapter 12, there are eight borderline chapters which could reasonably be interpreted either way.

When God changes Abram's name to Abraham and Jacob's to Israel, he does something only God can do, because for the Hebrews your name means not your social label but your divinely ordained nature, character and destiny. That's why Jesus was implicitly claiming divinity when he changed Simon's name to Peter (John 1:42).

The call of Abraham in Genesis 12 comes right after the Tower of Babel in chapter 11 to contrast man's way with God's way. The tower symbolizes all proud human attempts to conquer heaven and happiness by force, or to create a heaven on earth by cleverness (language, reason, science, technology). God's confusion of their language is like God's confusion of our technology: neither Tower of Babel reaches heaven and happiness, but only confusion (babble) and failure. Throughout the Bible, the symbolism remains the same: all human towers to heaven tumble, and all divine descents succeed. Our "way up" always turns out to be a "way down," and all divine "ways down" turn out to be the "way up." The Messiah is the prime example.

How reasonable the Tower of Babel sounds, and how silly the call of Abraham seems! What a way to fight the serious battle against evil—to pick out one man, flawed like all of us, for a lifelong trek into the wilderness with no road map and no guarantees, only promises. Yet this is the beginning of history's most public miracle: the Jewish people. Their survival and continued rejuvenation, their unparalleled flourishing and achievements, out of all proportion to their tiny size and strength, violate every known law of history and sociology. The more we consider their history, the more we are in awe at divine providence. The more we open our eyes to see, the more we open our mouths to gasp.

Consider just one incident in the long Joseph story, found in chapters 37 to 51. If one Egyptian tailor had not skimped on the thread of Joseph's mantle, no Jew would be alive today. That mantle came apart in the hands of Potiphar's wife, who was thus able to unjustly convict Joseph of attempted rape and get him imprisoned, where he met Pharaoh's butler and baker and interpreted their dreams, thus coming to Pharaoh's attention, interpreted *his* dreams, and saved Egypt from famine by his divine gift of prophecy. Only that grain preserved by Joseph's prophetic gift saved his family in Palestine who had sold him into slavery, when he finagled their coming to Egypt. Thus, generations later, we have hordes of healthy Jewish slaves in Egypt, ripe for Moses' liberation in the Exodus, and all their subsequent history.

In international diplomacy that divine technique is called brinkmanship. In chess, it's called a wild gambit. In gambling, it's called going against the odds. God's style is *not* conservative!

Notice how God uses his own enemy, evil, against itself and for good. The obvious lesson of the whole long story of Joseph and of all human history miniaturized here, is providence (see Romans 8:28). Or, as Joseph tells his brothers about their having sold him into slavery, "You meant evil against me but God meant it for good" (50:20). "God writes straight with crooked lines." That's how he redeemed the world—when Satan, Judas, Pilate, and Caiaphas conspired to crucify Christ and thus redeem the world!

God has nothing but flawed instruments to work with. There is a striking contrast between the heroes of *Genesis* and the heroes of pagan mythology. The men of the Bible are real: flawed, weak, stupid, sinful. Adam, Noah, Abraham, Isaac, Jacob, Moses—every one of them is a spiritual klutz, learning only through repeated mistakes. What makes them heroes is not their strength but their faith. They believe: that is, they let God be God, they open the door to the real power, the real success, which is God's activity, not their own.

We can all do that. Thus we can identify with these heroes,

as we can't identify with Hercules (unless we're Rambo) or Aphrodite (unless we're Marilyn Monroe).

A GOD OF INFINITE JUSTICE AND OF INFINITE LOVE

It's often said that the Old Testament, especially *Genesis*, teaches a God of wrath and justice, in stark contrast to Jesus, who teaches a God of forgiveness and love. It is a lie, of course. The God of the Old Testament does all that he does out of love; and the Father of Jesus needs to satisfy justice as well as love; that's why Jesus had to die. I used to think that only those who never read the Bible but read only silly secondary sources could fall for this fallacy. But experience has taught me otherwise; many students who read the Bible for the first time get this idea. Why?

I think it comes not only from the Gnostic heretics still very much among us, but also from misunderstanding the literary style of *Genesis*. It is not meant to be psychology, either of God or humanity. The modern style of storytelling emphasizes psychological motive and scrutinizes inner consciousness. This is simply not the style of premodern writing. Augustine's *Confessions* is the only personal introspective autobiography in pre-modern literature.

Thus the "wrath of God" is not meant as a description of God's own private feelings, but of his public deeds, of how those deeds look to fallen, "wrathful" man. Psychologically, this is "projection." When God gave Lady Julian of Norwich a "showing" of his wrath, she said, "I saw no wrath but on man's part."

God is indeed a God of justice and thus of punishment, which is part of justice. But love is the motive behind all his deeds of discipline. "For the Lord disciplines him whom he loves, . . . If you are left without discipline, then you are illegitimate children and not sons" (Hebrews 12:6-8).

Genesis is the book of beginnings, and no subsequent change in all human history ever has or ever will alter the essential pattern of the story begun here. Even a nuclear holocaust would be only Cain and Abel on a worldwide scale. Even the fall of Rome (i.e., of civilization) was only the Tower of Babel on a larger scale. God remains faithful, man remains faithless, God remains patient, man remains fickle, to the end—and God triumphs in the end. Paradoxically, the most human, humane, humanistic, humanly fulfilling thing man can say to God is: "Arise, O Lord! Let not man prevail, . . ." (Psalm 9:19). For we are our own worst enemies, and our divine opponent against whom we strive is our best friend and only hope.

Genesis ends with the chosen people in slavery, but it ends in hope. The Old Testament ends with a prophecy of warning and a curse (Malachi 4:6), but with hope for the Messiah. The New Testament ends with an apocalypse, but with hope: "Amen. Come, Lord Jesus!" No book is more severe *and* no book is more hopeful than the Bible, from *Genesis* on. Not the slightest compromise is made either with the optimistic pride that tries to recreate Eden or with the pessimistic despair that refuses to believe, to hope, and to love. *Genesis* destroys our two great illusions, if we let it. It is utterly unsparing. You cannot read it without being changed, if you let it interpret you before you interpret it.

FOUR

God's "Liberation Theology": Exodus

SUPERNATURAL LIBERATION FROM THE DEEPER SLAVERY OF SIN

Genesis was about a genesis: of creation, fall, and redemption. *Exodus*, not surprisingly, is about an exodus: of God's people from Egyptian slavery. The exodus was the event which, more than any other, forged the identity of the Jewish people, the event they looked back to for the next three thousand five hundred years as the decisive one in their history.

It is enlightening to contrast the way an orthodox Jewish or Christian theologian looks on this event with the way liberal or modernist theologians look at it, especially contemporary Christian "liberation theologians." For this difference about the past is reflected in a difference about the present, about what God is doing for us today, and how, essentially, we are supposed to work with him; what the essential *opus dei* or work of God is.

For the modernist, all the supernatural elements in the exodus, all the miracles, all the divine initiatives, are the Jewish people's retrospective interpretation of the historical

37

facts, not historical facts themselves. Piously desiring to give God credit for their liberation, the Jews invented specific miracle myths to symbolize the general truth of divine providence, such as the ten miraculous plagues or the miraculous parting of the Red Sea (or Reed Sea). They read their present subjective faith back into their past objective history.

This view is self-defeating, for it does not really give God credit for anything much at all. Not miracles, for one thing. And not for choosing the Jews. The Jewish notion of the "chosen people" is indeed the proud and elitist one that it seems to most modern egalitarians *if* it was the Jews' interpretation rather than God's literal choice—*if* they only used God as a mythic way of speaking about themselves. It is the supernatural idea that is the only humble idea.

The same dispute concerns contemporary "liberation theology." The issue is: what is God doing, most fundamentally, in the world today, and what are we supposed to be doing to cooperate with him? The liberal answer is: inspiring political leaders to liberate oppressed peoples, as he inspired Moses to liberate the Jews from Egypt. In other words, the earthly manna of political freedom, power, and prosperity—liberation from their opposites of slavery, weakness, and poverty—is the most important thing. The heavenly manna is only a man-made myth or symbol for that.

The orthodox answer of both Jews and Christians to the same question is: God is giving us heavenly manna of divine grace. That is our primary need. Man can liberate man from human slavery, but only God can liberate man from the deeper slavery of sin.

In the orthodox interpretation of the exodus, it was Moses' faith, not his political shrewdness or power, that opened the gate to God's miracle-working liberation. Machiavelli, who was probably an atheist as well as one of the first modernists, goes so far as to imply that Moses must have had superior *arms* to accomplish his remarkable success! (This involves a radical "reinterpretation" of the text, of course; but far be it from a modernist to bow in superstitious slavery before objective data!)

THE SYMBOLISM OF THE EXODUS STORY

However, there is symbolism in *Exodus*. Catholic theologians ever since the fathers of the church have seen in the historical, literal events of the exodus also an allegory. Christ, the new Moses, liberates his people, the church, the new Israel, from the spiritual slavery of sin and from the power of the world (symbolized by Egypt), which is under the dominion of Satan (symbolized by Pharaoh), through the sea (death) and the wilderness (purgatory) to the promised land (heaven). This symbolic reading of eight elements in the exodus story does not replace the literal and historical one, but is built on it.

Tragically, this rich, double-level way of thinking has nearly disappeared from modern consciousness and biblical scholarship. It is either/or, literal *or* symbolic today. Modernists favor symbolic interpretations, but only of the embarrassing (to them) miracle stories, and symbolic interpretations that end up with less, not more, than the obvious, common-sense reading. The orthodox reaction to modernism, especially among Protestants, has been to defend the truth of literal miracles and the accuracy of biblical history and to suspect symbolism. But it can be both. St. Thomas Aquinas explains the reason:

> The author of Holy Writ is God, in whose power it is to signify His meaning not by words only (as man also can do) but by things themselves. So, whereas in every other science things are signified by words, this science [theology] has the property that the things signified by

the words have themselves also a [symbolic] signification
. . . the spiritual sense, which is based on the literal and
presupposes it. *(Summa Theologica, I, 1, 10).*

Since God writes history as man writes words, the literal
events of history can be signs of other truths just as human
words are signs of things other than themselves.

Symbolic interpretation of historical facts was not invented by Aquinas; it is biblical. For example, St. Paul sees
the exodus as a symbol of baptism (Romans 6:2-3; 1
Corinthians 10:1-2), and the Passover (Exodus 12) as a
symbol of Christ (1 Corinthians 5:7). Though Christ is called
the "Paschal" lamb and Easter the "Paschal" feast in the
liturgy, most Catholics do not make the connection to the
Passover because they do not think symbolically about real,
historical events.

THE LAW: THE VERY HEART OF IT IS LOVE

The giving of the law in *Exodus* is as important as the
exodus itself. The law is the center of Judaism, which is more
a practical religion than a theological or creedal one;
orthopraxis (right action) is more central for Jews than
orthodoxy (right belief).

Again, orthodox and modernist accounts of the giving of
the law differ. The text, which gives the orthodox account,
credits *God* with inventing and giving the Ten Commandments. In fact, his was the very hand that chiseled them in
Moses' stone tablets. The modernist instead credits Moses
with these ten "good ideas" (which is like crediting the mail
carrier with writing your letters).

We can distinguish four different levels or areas of the law.
The law is like an onion; strip away the outer layers and you
find the inner. Most publicly and externally, there are many
civil laws regulating public social life. Second, there are

detailed *liturgical,* ceremonial laws regulating worship. Both of these levels of the law are specified in *Leviticus,* the next book.

Third, the *moral* law, the Ten Commandments, given in *Exodus,* is a far deeper level of law. Unlike the specifically Jewish civil and ceremonial laws, such as kosher foods and tithing, the commandments are for all people, all societies, and all times. Thus, though Christians are in no way bound by the Jewish ceremonial or civil laws (because they were all in some way symbolic of Christ or preparatory for Christ), we are still under the Ten Commandments in one way, though not under them in two other ways.

We are under them in that they express God's changeless demands for all of us, God's blueprint, God's idea for human living. But we are freed from the *curse* of the law by Christ's atoning death; that is, we are freed from God's eternal punishment for our disobedience. And we are freed, gradually, from our impotence to obey it, from slavery to sin, by the Holy Spirit. In other words, the Son justifies us and the Spirit sanctifies us. These are two new relationships to the law.

The heart of the law, its fourth and deepest aspect, is love (see Deuteronomy 6:5, the most familiar of all Jewish prayers, and Matthew 22:35-40). Christianity did not invent the idea that "love is the fulfillment of the law." Christ's law of love is not new, but old. He says so himself. Many Christians believe the implicitly antisemitic idea that Judaism is a religion of law, not love, and Christianity a religion of love, not law. No, Christ only highlighted what is already the heart of Judaism.

The good Jew *loves* the law (see Psalm 1:2; 119:97). The psalmists frequently express this spontaneous emotion, something we do not easily understand. For we think of the law only as an abstract formula, a verbal command. How can you love that? Furthermore, any law necessarily threatens us with punishment for disobedience, so we naturally fear it rather than love it. How can the law be loved?

The answer is that the law expresses God's will, and is thus the glue that binds us to God. It is *God* we love *via* the law. The good Jew, like the good Christian, sees behind the law to the lawgiver whose will is perfect love. Since God gave the law out of love, we can obey it and desire to obey it out of love. Law and love are not enemies but allies.

MOSES: THE MOST COMPLETE PREFIGUREMENT OF CHRIST

Exodus centers on Moses, greatest of all Jewish prophets, the man who spoke with God face to face and lived. Moses is as prominent and primary in Judaism as Mohammed is in Islam or as Confucius is in Confucianism. Yet his deepest significance is beyond Judaism: Moses symbolizes and foreshadows Christ. Let's look at some of the ways, some of the parallels between Moses and Christ.

1. Both were outsiders (Exodus 3:1-10; John 3:13).
2. Both received long training before their public ministry (Exodus 2:10; Luke 3:23).
3. Both performed many miracles (Exodus 7-14: John 3:2 and 21:25).
4. Both were preserved from an evil king's plot to murder them as babies (Exodus 2:2-10; Matthew 2:14-15; and Revelation 12:1-6 and 13-17).
5. Both stood up against masters of evil (Exodus 7:11; Matthew 4:1).
6. Both fasted for forty days (Exodus 34:28; Matthew 4:2).
7. Both controlled the sea (Exodus 14:21; Matthew 8:26).
8. Both fed a multitude of people (Exodus 16:15; Matthew 14:20-21).
9. Both showed the light of God's glory on their faces (Exodus 34:35; Matthew 17:2).
10. Both endured rebellion from their people (Exodus 15:24; John 5:45-47).

11. Both were scorned at home (Numbers 21:1; John 7:5).
12. Both saved their people by intercessory prayer (Exodus 32:32; John 17:9).
13. Both spoke as God's mouthpiece (Deuteronomy 18:18; John 7:16-17).
14. Both had seventy helpers (Numbers 11:16-17; Luke 10:1).
15. Both gave a law from a mountain (Exodus 20; Matthew 5-7).
16. Both established memorials (Exodus 12:14; Luke 22:19).
17. Both reappeared after death (Matthew 17:3; Acts 1:3).
18. Both were prophets, priests, and kings—the three most important positions of authority in the ancient world.
19. Both conquered the world, the flesh, and the devil.
20. Finally, both brought their people from slavery to freedom and to the promised land.

Moses is the most complete symbol or prefigurement of Christ in the Bible.

GOD REVEALS HIS OWN ESSENTIAL NAME

Exodus contains what is perhaps the most profound verse in the Bible, the most profound thing human ears have ever heard: the verse that reveals the essence of ultimate reality, the nature of God as expressed in his own true name. Remember that for the ancients your name revealed your nature, your essence. Exodus 3:14 is the only time God ever revealed his own essential name. All the other names for God in the Bible are our names for him, or designate his relations to us. Once and once only does God use his own name for himself, what he is in himself: when he tells it to Moses from the burning bush.

Why only to Moses? Men and women had been wondering what was the true name of God for centuries; why did only Moses find out? A rabbi once told me the answer to that question: because Moses was the only one practical enough to go straight to the horse's mouth: he asked! God was waiting around for centuries for someone to ask him; instead, they only speculated!

The divine name is simply "I AM," or "I AM WHO AM." It is the name Jesus appropriated for himself in John 8:58, thus clearly and uncompromisingly claiming divinity and inviting execution for blasphemy. For no Jew will ever even pronounce the divine name. In fact, no one even knows how to correctly pronounce it since it has not been pronounced for milennia. It was written only in consonants, omitting the vowels. Thus it is called the sacred Tetragrammaton or four-consonant, four-letter word, JHWH.

The reason no Jew will speak it is that, unlike any other name, you cannot say it without claiming to bear it. You can say "John" or "Mary" in the second or third person, but "I" only in the first. You can say "Hi, John" or "Have you seen Mary?" but you can't say "I" unless you *are* "I." God thus asserts his incommunicable, unique being, the divine subjectivity. He is not object but subject. As Buber says, "God cannot be expressed, only addressed." For "He is the Thou that cannot become an It."

That's why he always initiates rather than responding, questions rather than answering, knows rather than being known, wills the law rather than being under it, and impregnates our souls rather than vice versa. That is why "she" is a wrong symbol for him and "he" a right one. To the feminists' seemingly reasonable protests against the apparent male chauvinism in the Bible's language about God, we must reply, as C.S. Lewis says, simply: "God himself has taught us how to speak of him."

FIVE

God's Law, Israel's Wanderings, and Moses' Farewell: Leviticus, Numbers, and Deuteronomy

T HESE THREE BOOKS, coming after *Genesis* and *Exodus*, complete the Pentateuch, the five Books of Moses on which all of Judaism is based. Though not as richly varied as *Genesis* or *Exodus*, they contain priceless and unforgettable gems.

LEVITICUS: THE BOOK OF LAWS

The Hebrew title for this book is its first word, *Wayyiqra,* "and he called." God, not man, called into being these laws and their administrators, the Levites. The English title "Leviticus" means "the things of the Levites." *Leviticus* is the book of laws God gave Israel through Moses.

As Israel's law book, *Leviticus* contains hundreds of regulations extending to exact and tiny details of Israel's social life and temple worship. It is obviously *not* exciting reading, unless you happen to be a lawyer. Yet it is, when you realize that some extremely important lessons pervade all these minutiae:

1. God's loving care of his people reaches down into even the tiny details of their lives. Nothing is too small to be an occasion for his care or our obedience.

2. Law is good. It is not "repressive" of good, only of evil. God is the author of law and good order, not of confusion. He gives us law out of love for us, for our instruction, discipline, and protection.

3. The key word and idea in the book is *holiness*—a word which occurs over eighty times. The key text is 11:45: "I am the Lord who brought you up out of the land of Egypt, to be your God; you shall therefore be holy, for I am holy." That gives us our essential motive for sanctity.

4. The laws in *Leviticus* were God's gracious provision for sinful man to approach a holy God. Like the New Testament, *Leviticus* unites two apparently opposite ideas, law and grace, justice and mercy, the demand for obedience and the promise of forgiveness for disobedience. The God of *Leviticus* is both absolutely holy and absolutely loving, uncompromisingly just and uncompromisingly merciful.

5. Most important of all, *Leviticus* foreshadows Christ. The New Testament *Epistle to the Hebrews* interprets these laws messianically and symbolically. *Hebrews* should be read together with *Leviticus* as companion books.

St. Paul calls Israel's law "our tutor to bring us to Christ" (Galatians 3:24, NKJV). Christ's sacrifice on the cross and the presentation of this sacrifice in the Mass are symbolized and foretold by the offerings that made up Israel's temple liturgy: the holocaust or burnt offering foretold Christ's death, the peace offering foretold the peace Christ would make between God and rebellious man, and the sin offering foretold Christ as bearing the punishment for our sins.

Yom Kippur, the "Day of Atonement," was the most important day in the Hebrew calendar. On this day alone the high priest entered the Holy of Holies to make (or rather to foreshadow Christ's making) atonement ("at-one-ment," reconciliation) with God for the sins of his people (16:30). Aaron, the temporal high priest in *Leviticus*, foreshadows Christ our eternal high priest who offers himself to the Father for our salvation.

Why must Christ die to save us? Because the necessary penalty and consequence of sin, from the beginning, was death (Genesis 3:2). The bloody sacrifices in *Leviticus* were based on the principle that "the life of the flesh is in the blood; and I have given it for you upon the altar to make atonement for your souls; for it is the blood that makes atonement, by reason of the life" (17:11; see Hebrews 9:22). "For the wages of sin is *death*, but the free gift of God is eternal *life* in Christ Jesus our Lord" (Romans 6:23).

NUMBERS: ISRAEL'S WANDERINGS IN THE WILDERNESS

"In the wilderness" (Hebrew, *Bemidbar*), the fifth word of the book in Hebrew, is the usual Hebrew title of this book, because it is the story of Israel's wanderings in the wilderness, the desert of Sinai, between Egypt and the promised land. Moses kept a diary of these wanderings, according to 33:2, which leads many conservative or traditional Jews and Christians to believe that he was the author of this book, and of the rest of the Pentateuch, though the majority of Scripture scholars doubt this.

The English title, "Numbers," refers to the two times Moses took a numbering or census of all Israel. In chapter 1 he numbered the old generation that left Egypt, and in chapter 26 he numbered the new generation that was born in the wilderness and would enter the promised land. Only Joshua, along with Caleb, spans both generations. He and Caleb are the only Jews born in Egypt who were allowed to enter the promised land. The rest all refused to trust and obey God in the wilderness and when he commanded them to go ahead and conquer the land (chapter 14).

This is a painful book. In it Israel learns the hard lesson of
the unavoidable tragic consequences of unbelief and disobedience. It is a purgatorial education and purification,
necessary for a people not yet mature in faith and obedience.
It is fools, they say, who learn by experience.

Like *Leviticus, Numbers* teaches both the justice and the
mercy, both the severity and the kindness, of God. Despite
its painful lesson, it is an optimistic, upbeat book, for it
teaches that God's people (now as well as then) can move
forward to inherit God's promises (the promised land,
symbol of heaven) if and only if they learn the exceedingly
simple and therefore exceedingly difficult lesson to trust and
obey.

Christians find a number of symbols of Christ in *Numbers,*
including:

1. the bronze serpent on the stake (21:4-9), which symbolizes Christ on the cross (John 3:14);
2. the rock that quenched the people's thirst, which St.
   Paul interprets as Christ (1 Corinthians 10:4), for Christ
   and Christ alone satisfies all our heart's desires, that are
   restless till they rest in him;
3. the manna that came down from heaven (11:7-9), which
   symbolizes the Eucharist, Christ as the Bread of Life
   (John 6:31-33);
4. the cities of refuge (chapter 35), which symbolize the
   Sacrament of Reconciliation.

DEUTERONOMY: MOSES' FAREWELL SPEECHES

The Hebrew title, *Haddebharim,* "the words" (1:1), indicates
the central contents of this book: three long speeches by
Moses (1:1-4:43; 4:44-26:19; and 27-34) to prepare Israel for the
climax of the story of the exodus and their wanderings in the

wilderness: the conquest and inhabiting of the promised land.

Moses is 120 years old and about to die. This is his swan song, his farewell to the new generation written down for all generations. These are sermons not only for Israel but for all the "people of God," for the church. As *Leviticus* is the lawbook, *Deuteronomy* is the essential book of sermons. But while the laws were for Israel alone, the sermons are for all times and peoples.

The word "Deuteronomy" comes from the Greek word meaning "second law" because in this book the Ten Commandments are repeated a second time (chapter 5).

The essential point of all Moses' sermons is simple. It is the message of Psalm 1, the message of the two ways. Two and only two ways are open for us in this life: the way of obedience to God and the way of disobedience. These roads lead to two different destinations just as surely as two different physical roads lead to two different physical destinations. The way of obedience is divinely guaranteed to lead to inheriting all God's promises. The way of disobedience is equally guaranteed to result in tragedy and failure.

The history of Israel as recorded in the next twelve historical books of the Bible repeatedly and consistently illustrate and prove the truth of this central lesson. So does the history of every other nation and of every individual life throughout the history of the world.

The two most memorable and precious verses are:

1. the "shema" (6:4-5), the prayer that is to a Jew what the "Our Father" is to a Christian: "Hear, O Israel: The LORD our God is one LORD; and you shall love the LORD your God with all your heart, and with all your soul, and with all your might." Nothing, in time or eternity, is more important than that.

2. the fundamental challenge and choice that Moses

presents to Israel and that life presents to us: "I call heaven and earth to witness against you this day, that I have set before you life and death, blessing and curse; therefore choose life, that you and your descendants may live, loving the Lord your God, obeying his voice, and cleaving to him; for that means life to you" (30:19-20).

Because of Moses' disobedience (Numbers 20:7-13), God did not allow him to enter the promised land that he so longed for. Or rather, God postponed it until later, for when Moses appeared with Christ on the Mount of Transfiguration (Matthew 17:3) he was clothed with heavenly glory. The fact that Joshua (whose name is the same as Jesus) rather than Moses led Israel into the promised land symbolizes the fact that Moses is only a preparation for Christ, a kind of John the Baptist. Christ alone fulfills all the Old Testament symbols and types, especially that of Moses.

Moses was one of the greatest men who ever lived. The last three verses of *Deuteronomy* are a beautiful epitaph to this spiritual giant. (This epitaph, and the account of Moses' death in chapter 34, were obviously not written by Moses, even if the rest of the Pentateuch was, as the orthodox rabbinic tradition claims, but probably by Joshua.) Yet even this giant was a sinner and a failure without Christ. There's no more hope for Moses than for us; no less for us than for Moses.

SIX

From Conquest to Chaos: Joshua and Judges

Unlike *all* the other sacred Scriptures in the world, the Bible is *essentially* history. Though often interrupted by long stretches of sermon, song, poetry, prophecy, parables, wisdom, or laws, the unity and continuity of the Bible is its historical "story line." That story runs from the very beginning of time itself, in *Genesis,* to the end of time, in *Revelation.*

We are still in this same story. History is our story. It is also "his-story." God reveals himself and his wisdom not only through the words of the Bible but also through the events of history, just as through the things in nature. Since we are in this same story today and since it is "his-story," the principles and lessons that held true in the past eras, chronicled in Old Testament historical books like these, are just as true today. The lessons of these books are lessons of life-and-death importance for the survival of America, of Russia, of Upper Volta, as much as for ancient Israel. For the laws of history do not change, any more than the laws of nature do.

The Bible is "sacred history." That does not mean anything less realistic than secular history, as some modern theologians imply—as if "Bible stories" belonged to the category of myths or fairy tales. Rather, "sacred history" means history from a double point of view, the divine as well as the human. It has two natures. Like Jesus, the Bible is "the Word of God" in the words of man. Its human nature is not suppressed but added to by its divine nature.

The history of God's chosen people, ancient Israel, is full of divinely revealed secrets about national life and death, about the secret of survival and salvation socially as well as individually. No book of social, political, or historical science has ever shown more clearly how nations rise and fall, succeed and fail, by using or refusing their lifeline to God, the source of all life, this-worldly as well as other-worldly and social as well as individual. For Israel's history is the key to the world's. Israel is not God's exception but God's rule, God's universal paradigm case.

JOSHUA: A CALL TO FOLLOW OUR COMMANDER AND ENGAGE IN SPIRITUAL WARFARE

The *Book of Joshua* is the end of one story and the beginning of another. It is the happy ending to the long epic of Israel's deliverance from Egypt and slavery and the fulfillment of God's promise to Abraham back in *Genesis*: the "promised land." It is also the beginning of the hard tale of the conquest of that land.

As such, it is a warlike, grisly book, full of blood and violence. We tend to turn away from such a warlike book today, giving the apparently good reason that the Prince of Peace has come, and God no longer commands his people to fight bloody wars as he did then. But we are just as much at war now as then. Spiritual warfare will never end until the end; and this warfare is just as real, just as awful and as awe-full, as physical warfare. For who, after all, are more grisly: Canaanite generals or demons?

Yet this idea of spiritual warfare, so prominent in Scripture and the lives of the saints, is rarely taught today. We forget that "we are not contending against flesh and blood, but against the principalities, against the powers, against the world rulers of this present darkness, against the spiritual hosts of wickedness in the heavenly places" (Ephesians 6:12). The life-or-death battles in the old covenant, especially in this most warlike book, are apt symbols of the no less life-or-death spiritual warfare of the New.

The simple success strategy of God's people in *Joshua* is the old lesson of "trust and obey" (good military wisdom, if your commander is perfect!). Whenever Israel trusts and obeys her divine commander, she triumphs, even against apparently unconquerable obstacles, such as the Jordan River, which is miraculously crossed (chs. 3-4), and the walls of Jericho, which "come tumblin' down" (ch. 6).

Like any general, God leads through different paths. Sometimes he leads his people through miracles, sometimes not. Sometimes his orders make human, rational sense, like the military strategy of "divide and conquer"; but sometimes they seem sheer folly to human prudence, like the command to march seven times around Jericho blowing trumpets. Why does God act in such an apparently arbitrary way?

The appearance of arbitrariness and irrationality is an echo, a projection of our own expectations and categories onto God. God acts in humanly irrational ways for a very good reason: to test his people and teach them the crucial lesson that "some boast of chariots, and some of horses; but we boast of the name of the LORD our God. They will collapse and fall; but we shall rise and stand upright" (Psalm 20:7-8); the lesson that "Unless the Lord builds the house, those who build it labor in vain" (Psalm 127:1). God is never arbitrary; he always has good reasons, but they appear arbitrary to us because they are so much better than ours.

The *Book of Joshua* centers around the hero of its title. It traces his life from the beginning of his public leadership, which he inherited from Moses, right up to his final farewell speech and death, which are strikingly similar to Moses' final speech and his death at the end of *Deuteronomy*. Joshua is the new Moses.

But isn't it Jesus who is the new Moses? Yes. And the Hebrew spelling of "Jesus" is "Yeshua," which is the same as "Joshua." Moses gave him this name (Numbers 13:16), changing his original name, "Hoshea," which means "salvation," to "Yehoshua" ("Joshua"), which means "The Lord is salvation."

The church has traditionally interpreted Joshua as a type or symbol of Jesus for at least six reasons:

1. The name and its meaning are the same;
2. Jesus, like Joshua, is the new Moses;
3. He is the commander of God's chosen people and the conqueror of God's enemies;
4. He is the one who leads his people even through the waters of death (symbolized by the Jordan River in *Joshua* and the water of baptism in the New Testament—see Romans 6:4);
5. He does what Moses could not do: he brings his people into the promised land (symbolic of heaven);
6. Further, the conquest and division of the land into the twelve tribes symbolizes and foreshadows the expansion of Christ's church into the world by his twelve apostles.

But the thing symbolized is always more than the symbol. Christ, the new Joshua, did what the old Joshua could not do: save his people forever, not just for a time; and from spiritual defeat (sin), not just from military defeat.

There are many memorable events in this book, so vivid that children remember them almost as well as the events in *Genesis,* once they hear them. But two passages stand out as especially significant. In the first, a heavenly figure appears who is called "the commander of the Lord's army" (5:13-15). Some commentators think this is not just Michael the archangel, but Christ himself in pre-incarnate form.

In the most important passage of all (24:15), Joshua calls upon all Israel to make *the* great choice, the single greatest choice every individual and society must make in his, her, or their life, because this choice determines the meaning and purpose and point of life itself, and even determines life or death for eternity: "Choose this day whom you will serve, whether the gods your fathers served in the region beyond the river, or the gods of the Amorites in whose land you dwell; but as for me and my house, we will serve the Lord."

It is a perfect echo of Deuteronomy 30:15-19, where Moses, in *his* farewell sermon, confronts us with the same choice. The bloody, death-threatening militarism of *Joshua* boils down to this Mosaic wisdom: "Choose life."

JUDGES: ISRAEL'S REPEATED FAILURES AND GOD'S REPEATED DELIVERANCE

During the four centuries between the death of Joshua and the age of the Kings (beginning with Saul, David, and Solomon), Israel was ruled by a series of seventeen judges. These were not just judges in the modern sense, that is administrators of legal justice, but also political governors and military leaders. Most were warriors (for example, Samson and Gideon), one was a priest (Eli), and one was a prophet (Samuel). Prophets, priests, and kings (rulers) were the three most important offices God appointed for his people, and all three point to Christ, who is the ultimate prophet (the very Word of God), priest (mediator and Savior), and king (ruler of the whole cosmos). The Hebrew word for "judge," *shophet*, also means "savior" or "deliverer," just as "Jesus" does.

If *Joshua* is the book of repeated successes, *Judges* is the book of repeated failures. Israel's history during this time is a dark age full of corruption, a large black sky with only a few bright stars. For after Joshua and the generation that had conquered the promised land with him had died out, "There arose another generation after them, who did not know the Lord" (2:10).

Judges contains seven cycles of Israel's disobedience and repentance, infidelity and return to fidelity to God. Again and again, Israel compromises and worships the gods of the native Canaanites—just as we, the New Israel, worship the gods of our society (consumerism, control, comfort, power, prestige, pleasure). Again and again, the loss of Israel's inner, spiritual strength results in a loss of outer, material strength socially, politically, and militarily; and they are defeated and oppressed. Compromise always leads to chaos.

Then they repent, and God raises up a new judge each time to deliver them. (No amount of human folly can exhaust the divine patience.) But each new judge-deliverer is different. The monotony of Israel's (and our) sins contrasts with the creative originality of God's methods of deliverance: Samson, Gideon, Samuel.

The stories are both vividly realistic and vividly "numinous": awesome, arresting. If these stories are myths rather than history, then a whole genre of modern literature, realistic fantasy—almost science fiction—was invented three thousand years before it ever appeared again in the world's literature!

Alas, as soon as Israel is delivered, prosperity leads to

pride and disobedience once again, and the endless cycle repeats itself:

All human history, individual and social, follows this pattern. And its fundamental lesson, the simplest lesson we have ever been taught, "trust and obey," turns out to be the hardest one for us to remember and practice. It has to be lost and found time after time.

The story is utterly up-to-date. The history of nations ever since Israel has continued to teach the sad results of "playing God." The last verse of the book sums it up and reveals the root cause of Israel's ills: "every man did what was right in his own eyes" (21:25).

How relevant is this old book to us? The degree of its relevance is exactly proportionate to how little we fear "every man doing what is right in his own eyes." Does this sound to us like a recipe for disaster or for mental maturity, health, and wholeness? Is this not the basic advice of nearly all our psychological "sages" today? Are there many leaders in our society who believe, preach, and practice the opposite of "every man doing what is right in his own eyes"?

That unfashionable opposite is summarized simply in

Proverbs 3:5-7:

> Trust in the LORD with all your heart,
> and do not rely on your own insight.
> In all your ways acknowledge him,
> and he will make straight your paths.
> Be not wise in your own eyes;
> fear the LORD, and turn away from evil.

There's no other way than these two.

SEVEN

National Happiness from Personal Holiness: First and Second Samuel

T HE HISTORICAL BOOKS of the Bible were not designed, either by men or by God, merely to satisfy our natural curiosity about past events, but to guide our present lives and choices to ensure our future supernatural blessedness. To look for "lessons" in these books, therefore, is not an arbitrary imposition of an external, alien point of view. For God, unlike human beings, writes lessons not only in words but also in events. He is the primary author of the book of history as well as of these historical books.

There are many memorable "lessons" in *First* and *Second Samuel*. (How naive, unfashionable, and "moralistic" the very word "lesson" sounds to our modern ears! In that psychological fact itself there lies a lesson.) Among them, one of the most prominent and relevant to our own time is the dependence of a nation's happiness on its leaders' personal holiness.

First and *Second Samuel* contrast the personalities of good but weak Eli with good and strong Samuel, strong but selfish Saul with idealistic David, David as obedient with

David as disobedient; and they show how these contrasts, these choices, will determine all of Israel's subsequent history. The difference between a two-degree angle and a three-degree angle is perhaps only a fraction of an inch in the beginning, close to its origin. But when the lines are extended through space, as history is extended through time, the difference becomes a matter of many feet and eventually miles.

First Samuel traces Israel's history from the birth of Samuel, last of the judges, to the death of Saul, Israel's first king. Second Samuel traces the rule of David, Israel's second and greatest king.

FIRST SAMUEL: THE AGE OF KINGSHIP EMERGES

Samuel, the last judge, anoints Saul, the first king. A new age emerges through this transition. "Anointing" was a quasi-sacramental, symbolic pouring of oil onto the head of the man God chose. It publicly signified and certified God's choice. The title "Christ" or "Messiah" means "the anointed one" or "the chosen one." The Jewish kings as God's chosen ones and the Jews as God's "chosen people" foreshadow and prepare for Christ, God's Chosen Person.

Before the transition from Samuel to Saul, we see a transition from Eli, the old priest, to Samuel, the young prophet. At a time when "the word of the LORD was rare in those days; there was no frequent vision" (3:1), God called Samuel, dramatically but quietly, in the night. And Samuel gave the perfect, classic response to God's call, just as Mary was to do one thousand years later with her "fiat." Samuel said simply, "Speak, Lord, for thy servant hears" (3:9). Only because Samuel first listened to God, did Israel listen to Samuel: "When Samuel spoke, all Israel listened" (3:21, TEV). This is *the* key to all effective preaching, priesting, and pastoring.

The people asked Samuel for a king, "like all the nations" (8:5). Like us modern Americans, they didn't want to be different. This disappointed God (God is not an American), but God let them have their foolish way (8:6-9) to teach them—the hard way.

They chose Saul as their king, not for his wisdom or holiness but for his "image," as we would put it today: "There was not a man among the people of Israel more handsome than he. . . . he was taller than any of the people" (9:2).

The time of Saul, like most times, was full of corruption. Eli's wicked sons, ruling at Shiloh, were so bad that God sent terrible judgment on the nation. Israel was defeated in battle by the Philistines (ch. 4). Eli's sons were killed. And Eli died in grief and horror at hearing that the ark of the covenant, God's visible throne in Israel and the holiest object in the world, was captured. It was almost as if a Satanist were to steal the Eucharist for a Black Mass. Eli's daughter-in-law died in childbirth upon hearing the news, and named her son "Ichabod," which means "the glory has departed."

But Saul was not the answer to the departed glory. Though for a time he gave Israel military glory and victory, he proved to be an evil king (13:8-14; 15:10-23; 28:3-17). He was envious of David and sought to murder him, even though David was God's anointed.

David was protected from Saul by his friend Jonathan, Saul's son and heir. The friendship between David and Jonathan is the classic, model friendship. Jonathan gave up to David his legitimate claim to be king (20:30-31) because of his loyalty to David and because of his loyalty to God, for he knew God had chosen David to be king (ch. 18).

The crisis and culmination of Saul's dissolution and self-destruction came when he played with the occult—something God had forbidden with frightening strictness (Exodus 22:18; Deuteronomy 18:9-12). Once Saul conjured up the spirit of the dead prophet Samuel through the mediumship of the Witch of En-Dor (ch. 28), it was too late: Saul lost his kingdom, his life, and perhaps his soul. Samuel told him, "The LORD has turned from you and become your enemy" (28:16; compare Matthew 7:23). Saul's story is a story of crime and punishment, a moral tragedy.

SECOND SAMUEL: ISRAEL'S BRIEF GOLDEN AGE

But David's story is one of glory. David is Israel's model king, the standard all subsequent kings are judged by. David is one of the primary Old Testament types or symbols for Christ:

1. He is a king;
2. He is born in Bethlehem;
3. He is anointed ("Christ");
4. He is "a man after God's own heart" (1 Samuel 13:14);
5. He experiences rejection and danger, and out of it composes some of the great messianic psalms, such as the one (Psalm 22) Jesus quoted on the cross;
6. He is the literal ancestor of Christ, who is frequently called "the son of David" and "descended from David according to the flesh" (Romans 1:3);
7. And like Christ, David forgives and spares his enemies. On two occasions, he spared Saul's life when Saul was seeking his (chs. 24-26).

King David is a type of Christ the King. It is difficult for us Americans to love kings, for our nation was born in a rebellion against a bad king. Yet Christ *is* a king as well as prophet and priest. The church has not designed for us "the Feast of Christ the President," but the Feast of Christ the King. Christ did not preach "the administration of God," but "the kingdom of God."

God promised David through Nathan the prophet that

the Messiah would be descended from him. This hope for an even greater king than David was kept alive in Israel during the dark times of decline, corruption, civil war, exile, and captivity that were to follow for many long generations after David. The New Testament refers to Nathan's prophecy and Christ's fulfillment of it three times (Acts 2:30; 2 Corinthians 6:18; and Hebrew 1:5). David is the connecting hinge between Abraham, who first received the promise, and Christ, who finally fulfilled it; he is halfway between Abraham (about 2000 B.C.) and Christ.

David wanted to build God's house, the temple, but God decreed that it should be built instead by David's son Solomon, a man of peace. David wanted to build a house for God, but instead God built a house for David. The "house of David" is a dynasty divinely guaranteed to produce not just a great temporal kingdom but an eternal one (see Luke 1:32-33). The prophecy was fulfilled: David's dynastic line was preserved right down to the time of the Messiah, who was David's great-great-great-etc.-grandson. In the northern kingdom of Israel there were nine different family dynasties, but in Judah only one. Judah was the only tribe (with Benjamin) that remained until the time of Christ; the other ten were scattered and lost.

The characters of Eli, Samuel, Saul, Nathan, and David are vivid and memorable because they are realistic. Though David is Israel's greatest king and a type of Christ, *Second Samuel* does not idealize him or gloss over his sins.

Second Samuel tells David's story as both history and biography. For the fate of the nation and of David are intertwined. The spiritual law of cause and effect is seen not only individually but also socially. David's spiritual success brought about God's blessing not only in his private life, but also in the life of the nation; and David's spiritual failures necessarily brought down God's judgment not only on him and his family, but also on his nation.

David's remarkable political "rags to riches" story (from

shepherd boy to king) and his remarkable military success in quenching civil war and enforcing peace stemmed from his personal friendship with God and obedience to God's will. Then came the turning point in his life: his adultery with Bathsheba and his arranging the murder of her husband Uriah. The book then chronicles the tragic consequences of these sins for his family and for the nation.

These consequences start to unravel when Bathsheba's new baby by David dies shortly after birth. Later one of David's sons, Amnon, commits incest with his half-sister Tamar. Then David's beloved son Absalom, the full blood brother of Tamar, murders his half-brother Amnon to avenge his sister, leads a military revolt against his father David, and is killed by David's general Joab. One of the most poignantly agonizing passages in the Bible is David's grief over Absalom: "O my son Absalom, my son, my son Absalom! Would I had died instead of you, O Absalom, my son, my son!" (18:33).

Nathan's prophecy is fulfilled: God sends a sword into David's house. Not only family disaster but also national disaster come: famine, war with Philistia, and, later, the renewed civil war under Solomon's sons that would split Israel forever.

The brief "Golden Age" Israel enjoyed lasted only one or two generations: part of David's rule and part of Solomon's. The rest is troubled times. Saul began in glory but ended in ruin. So did Solomon. Only David remained God's man, through repentance. David did not attain the best thing, personal purity and perfection, but he attained the next best thing, repentance. This was crucial for the nation. David's repentance held Israel together and staved off God's judgment for another generation.

One of the most arresting passages in Scripture is the scene of this repentance. Nathan the prophet confronts David with his crimes by his parable of the rich man who stole the poor man's single sheep. David is impaled by its stunning punch line: "You are the man." After reading 2

Samuel 12:1-15, read Psalm 51, the great prayer of repentance that David wrote after this. It is a favorite of many of the saints, for all saints know themselves to be sinners, and this is the great sinner's Psalm.

Here are four short and simple lessons for our time and our nation from *First* and *Second Samuel*.

1. *Most* times are times of trouble. Prosperity and peace are the exception, not the rule.

2. Personal sins produce national tragedies. Just as the sins of the fathers have consequences in the lives of their children (Exodus 20:5-6), the sins of the rulers have consequences in the life of the nation. This law does not change when kings change to presidents.

3. There exists an unavoidable law of spiritual cause and effect, as universal and as objective as the law of gravity: the only road to blessing is obedience, and the road to judgment is disobedience to God's laws.

4. But it's never too late. David's repentance restored him to God's favor, and although the sword remained in his house as a purgatorial punishment, David remained God's man. He weakened his relationship with God by sin, but did not destroy it, and restored it by repentance. If even a murderer and adulterer could be a great king and a great man of God, what can you be?

EIGHT

From Israel's Golden Age to Decline and Fall: First and Second Kings

T HE TWO *BOOKS OF KINGS,* originally one in the Jewish canon, trace the history of Israel from its peak, the reign of Solomon, through its decline, division, civil war, corruption, exile, and destruction.

FIRST KINGS: SOLOMON'S REIGN IS THE SUMMIT OF ISRAEL'S GOLDEN AGE

The Bible calls Solomon the greatest king in human history and the wisest man in the world, for his wisdom was not just from his humanity, but from God. This is clear at the beginning of his reign (ch. 3), when God promises Solomon any one gift, and he asks for wisdom—such a wise choice that it proves that he already has the wisdom he asks for:

"I am but a little child; I do not know how to go out or come in. . . . Give thy servant therefore an understanding mind to govern thy people" (3:7, 9).

God is so pleased that he gives Solomon not only the

wisdom he asked for, but also the riches, power, and honor he had not asked for. Under Solomon, Israel amassed unsurpassed riches and territory from the border of Egypt to the border of Babylonia. Best of all, an oasis of peace prevailed between the constant warfare before and after Solomon.

C.S. Lewis speaks of "Solomon—the bright solar blend of king and lover and magician which hangs about that name." But it is wisdom for which this archetypal king is most renowned. Immediately after Solomon asks for and receives the gift of wisdom from God, this wisdom is tested and shown by his judgment between two women who have equal claims on the same baby (ch. 3). Solomon turns the situation around: instead of being tested by the situation and the women, he tests them to discover which one is the real mother, just as Jesus did whenever he was apparently trapped by his interlocutors. Compare 1 Kings 3:16-28 with John 8:2-11.

This is the kind of wisdom we expect from God, who is the questioner, not the questioned, the First Person Singular ("I AM"). It is a wisdom mere human reason and education cannot teach, and it produced awe and wonder: "And Israel heard of the judgment which the king had rendered; and they stood in awe of the king, because they perceived that the wisdom of God was in him" (3:28). Just as Solomon's wisdom was first manifested in his asking God for wisdom, Israel's wisdom is manifested in their recognition of Solomon's wisdom.

For centuries after Solomon, anonymous Jewish writers often signed their books "Solomon." Solomon probably wrote most of *Proverbs*. But the writers of *Song of Songs*, *Ecclesiastes*, and *Wisdom of Solomon*, all of whom call themselves Solomon, all very probably wrote centuries later, using Solomon's name to indicate their teacher and model.

Jewish tradition has it that Solomon wrote *Song of Songs* in his youth, *Proverbs* in middle age, and *Ecclesiastes* in old age.

For *Song of Songs* idealistically exalts young love; *Proverbs* is the practical wisdom of maturity; and *Ecclesiastes* manifests the disillusionment of Solomon's old age when he had lost his wisdom and turned away from its source, "the fear of the Lord, the beginning of wisdom."

One of the most remarkable aspects of Solomon's wisdom was his ability to handle wealth without being corrupted by it. This is certainly an art that is rare and relevant today.

The first thing Solomon did with his wealth was to build God's house, the great temple. Like a medieval cathedral, it was a labor of love. Into it was poured a great deal of time and money, and (much more important) great passion and commitment. The Israelites considered this the richest and most beautiful building in the world, the best that man could do, for it was for God. The destruction of this temple was more traumatic to the Jews than most of us can realize. The second, rebuilt temple was also destroyed, by the Romans in A.D. 70. Only the "Wailing" (West) Wall is left: the most sacred place on earth for Jews. The rebuilding of the temple (of which we are now beginning to hear the first faint rumblings and hints) is supposed to be a sign of the end of the world and the coming of the Messiah.

In God's providential plan, Solomon's temple had to be great because it was a symbol of Christ, who compared his body to the temple when he said, "Destroy this temple, and in three days I will raise it up" (John 2:19). The temple had to be perfect because it was to receive the Messiah. It was like Mary's womb that way.

The symbol pales, however, before the reality symbolized. Thus Christ also said, "I tell you, something greater than the temple is here" (Matthew 12:6). In heaven, he will be our temple: "And I saw no temple in the city, for its temple is the Lord God the Almighty and the Lamb" (Revelation 21:22).

In his later life, Solomon's pagan wives turned his heart away from worshiping God to worshiping idols, and the king with the divided heart left behind him a divided kingdom. Solomon sunk into an orgy of idolatry pandering to all his wives, he worshiped all their gods as well as the Lord. He had a harem of three hundred wives by one count, seven hundred by another. Solomon made three mistakes: 1.) too many women, 2.) too many gods, and 3.) most importantly, he let his women choose his gods rather than letting his God choose his women.

After Solomon's death, civil war split the nation in two under his unwise son Rehoboam. (Unfortunately, wisdom is not hereditary.) Never again would Israel attain peace, glory, riches, or even unity as it had under Solomon. It was split forever, and eventually taken captive and enslaved. Like Camelot, Israel's golden age was like one brief summer.

First Kings is not a biography of the kings, nor is it a political history, but a spiritual history. Politically important kings, like Omri, are sometimes passed over quickly. Like *First* and *Second Samuel, First* and *Second Kings* is a prophetic interpretation of the invisible spiritual causes that led to the visible political decline and fall of Israel. It is a historical commentary on the first, greatest, and most practical commandment (Deuteronomy 6:5; Matthew 22:38). Once Israel favors other gods, God favors other nations. Nations can no more escape the moral and spiritual order than individuals can. God has no double standard.

SECOND KINGS: A DIVIDED ISRAEL LOSES ITS WAY

First Kings ends with Israel divided into two nations, after the civil war between Solomon's sons. *Second Kings* traces the history of both kingdoms down the slippery slope to destruction. Chapters 1-17 are confusing because they trace *two* sets of kings, alternately, in the two kingdoms of Israel and Judah. The northern kingdom was destroyed by Assyria in 722 B.C. (ch. 17), and Judah by Babylon in 586 B.C. (ch. 25).

Nineteen consecutive evil kings rule in Israel. All worship idols at Bethel. There are nine separate dynasties, and eight of them come to power by murdering the previous king.

In Judah there is only one dynasty, the house of David, which God promised would last until the Messiah. Eight of Judah's twenty kings are good, and Judah lasts one hundred thirty-six years longer than Israel. These two facts are interpreted as cause and effect by the prophetic author (who, by the way, may well have been the great prophet Jeremiah; the literary styles are similar).

But even Judah's good kings did not abolish idol worship. Therefore God abolished temple worship by allowing Nebuchadnezzar to destroy the temple and the holy city of Jerusalem. Once the temple no longer hosted the worship of the true God, it was no longer divinely preserved.

The remnant of the Jews, having lost their nation, their freedom, their holy city, and their temple, are marched nine hundred miles away into exile in Babylon. Read Psalm 137 to see how they felt.

During the period between Solomon and the exile (the period of the divided kingdom), most of the great prophets lived and taught: Elijah, Elisha, Amos, and Hosea in Israel; Isaiah, Jeremiah, Joel, Obadiah, Micah, Nahum, Zephaniah, and Habakkuk in Judah. The nation's spiritual health depended on heeding the Word of God through these divine mouthpieces, and the nation's bodily, political health, in turn, depended on its spiritual health. The same is true today of the church and the world—unless the church is *not* God's mouthpiece, God's public prophet.

TWO GREAT PROPHETS FORESHADOW JOHN THE BAPTIST AND CHRIST

In *First Kings* and *Second Kings,* we see the ministry of Elijah, one of the greatest prophets of all time. In the New

Testament he is a type or symbol of John the Baptist, whom Jesus calls the greatest of all (Matthew 11:11, 14). Like Christ, Elijah ascended to heaven (in a chariot of fire), and appeared on the Mount of Transfiguration with Moses (Matthew 17). Moses' death was also unusual since God buried him and his body was never found (Deuteronomy 43:6).

But Elisha, Elijah's successor, was a little more like Christ. Elijah lived alone like John the Baptist; Elisha lived among the people like Christ. Elijah emphasized law, repentance, and judgment, like John the Baptist; Elisha spoke more of faith, grace, and hope, like the gospel.

Among the many striking incidents in the lives of these two prophets, I am especially struck by Elisha's ability to see angels, the army of the Lord surrounding the army of Israel's enemies which surrounded Israel (2 Kings 7:13-17). It is a vision we certainly need to recapture today.

Second Kings ends on a note of hope, despite the terrible final chapter which describes the utter destruction of Jerusalem and the temple. Though God's chosen nation is ruined, God's plans are not. As in Noah's time, a small faithful remnant always remains. The Jews have a legend that there are twelve good men alive at every time in history; they save the world from God's judgment. God would have spared Sodom for only ten; perhaps just one more is all that is needed to spare America.

Even when sin seems to have the last word, it does not. God does. As St. Thomas More said, in a tumultuous time like Israel's and like ours, "The times are never so bad that a good man cannot live in them."

NINE

A Different Perspective on History: First and Second Chronicles

T HE LAST TIME I tried to read the Bible straight through, I bogged down somewhere in *Chronicles*. I think other readers have often had the same experience. And thereby hangs a tale—a fascinating tale about why we do not find *Chronicles* fascinating, as did those who wrote it and read it in premodern times.

THE FOUR DISTINCTIVES OF THE POINT OF VIEW IN CHRONICLES

First and *Second Chronicles* (originally one book, in the Jewish canon) tells the same story as the two books of *Samuel* and *Kings:* the story of all the kings of Israel, from Saul to the exile and captivity. But it tells the story from a different point of view and perspective, one we moderns find it hard to "identify with." There are four distinctive features of this point of view in *Chronicles*.

First, it is a more divine, less human and empirical point of view. It is a more "judgmental" book than *Samuel* or *Kings* because God has a right and a power to judge events beyond the little bit we have.

Second, it is a more priestly point of view, rather than a prophetic one. The prophet Samuel is traditionally thought to have written *Samuel*, but the priest Ezra may have written *Chronicles*. That would explain why *Chronicles* emphasizes the building of the temple, in great, even excruciating detail, and why its standard of judgment for evaluating each of the kings is whether he fostered, neglected, or opposed temple worship according to the Levitical priestly laws.

Third, it begins with nine whole chapters of genealogies. (Imagine *that* being read at Mass; it would double the population of sleepers.)

Fourth, it idealizes. It emphasizes the good kings more than the evil ones, the two best kings, David and Solomon most of all, the virtues and successes of David and Solomon rather than their faults and failures, and it tells only of Judah, the more faithful and longer-lasting kingdom, which contained the temple and had at least some good kings, while ignoring the history of the northern kingdom of Israel, the apostate and therefore shorter-lived kingdom, which had no temple and no good kings.

Now the fact that these four distinctive features of *Chronicles* make it less interesting than the previous historical books to the typically modern mind, even the modern Christian mind, tells us four interesting things about us and our mind. Becoming aware of these four typically modern habits of mind by contrast with this ancient book, criticizing them, and perhaps even reversing them (if we are both willing and able to do so), might go a long way toward healing four spiritual ills of our age and our mind. Thus the very irrelevance of *Chronicles* may turn out to make it extremely relevant to us. Let's explore how.

First, I wonder how much we Christians are unconsciously affected by the modern suspicion of the claim that the Bible is divine revelation, not just human wisdom; God's Word to man, not just man's words about God. If we did *not* share that suspicion, at least unconsciously, why would we not *prefer* a book like this, written from a more divine and heavenly point of view, over one written from a more earthly and empirical point of view, like *Samuel* or *Kings?*

Second, we favor the prophetic over the priestly point of view and emphasis. Perhaps this is because we like to emphasize morality, the special province of the prophet, more than liturgy and worship, the special province of the priest. We like to emphasize our "horizontal" duties to each other (ethics) more than our "vertical" duties to God (religion). Modernity tends to reduce supernatural religion to natural morality.

Why? I can think of at least two reasons. First, the moralities of the world are essentially the same, but the religions of the world are essentially different. Thus the belief and practice of one religion entails the unpopular judgment that other religions are false, or at least less true. Second, we know that morality concerns us, but we are not as convinced that temple worship concerns us. If the details of the building of Solomon's temple in Jerusalem which tend to bore us when we read *Chronicles* were details of our own home, or vacation cottage, we would be fascinated. This means that we do not really "identify with," and perhaps do not understand, the importance of the temple in Jerusalem, and its connection with Christ and thus with ourselves. (More about this later.)

Third, we are bored with the genealogies of *Chronicles* because we are out of touch with history, tradition, and our roots in the past. Or perhaps because we no longer believe that individuals (the names in the genealogies) can make much of a difference to history. The "Great Man" theory of history is nearly always scornfully rejected today. Christ himself is often seen as limited and conditioned by his times and culture.

The first nine chapters of *First Chronicles* consist of a long list of names going back to Adam. The ancients were fascinated with this sort of thing because they loved to remember and venerate their ancestors, from whom they had received a tradition they thought precious, even divine; also they saw names as sacred words, not mere labels. Remember the scene near the end of Alex Haley's "Roots," where the freed blacks, entering their new "promised land," recite their history and genealogy, beginning with their African ancestor Kunta Kinte.

Both the genealogies and the history in *Chronicles* focus on Judah, not Israel, because God's promise, as far back as Genesis 49:10, was that the Messiah would come from that tribe. In the Hebrew Bible, *Chronicles* is the last book. That's why the New Testament opens, in *Matthew*, with the genealogy of the Messiah: to show Christ as the fulfillment of the Old Testament prophecies and promises. This promise kept the Jews' spirit alive even when the body of their nation was dead or dying.

Finally, our fourth reason for disliking *Chronicles* is its idealism. We are more convinced of evil than of good. Certainly, we find evil more *interesting* than good. Virtues seldom make headlines; vices do. We demand "realism" in our histories and biographies, not "idealism."

Chronicles is idealistic, positive, and hopeful even though its times were miserable. Its readers were a poor, small, weak, straggling remnant of Jews just returned from captivity in Babylon to a ruined homeland and temple. It was probably written by Ezra, the priest-scribe, to encourage the people of Judah to rebuild the temple and to hope for a restoration of her past glories, to look back to their golden age and to look up to David and Solomon as imitable models, recoverable ideals—to be proud of their national heritage.

THE LESSON OF CHRONICLES

The pride was not to be national first of all, but spiritual. Ezra wanted to make sure his people's hope was in the proper order, the only truly practical and workable order: namely, that material hopes and glories are consequent and dependent on the spiritual. Thus *Chronicles* repeats the constant, and constantly forgotten, lesson of all Old Testament history: the nation's political health depends on its spiritual health, and the nation's spiritual health depends on the spiritual health of its leaders.

The gospel, or good news, of *Chronicles*, is the same as that of Moses: the covenant is a divinely guaranteed light even in the worst darkness, a hope beyond worldly wisdom. This hope was not a mere *wish*, but a *"sure and certain* hope of resurrection" of the glory of the Jewish nation, for it was based on God's guarantee, the promise of the one who cannot but keep his promises.

But the covenant has two parts. The promise is conditional. God fulfills his part only when his people fulfill theirs. The prophetic and moral lesson Ezra the priest finds in his people's history implicitly appeals to free will, free choice. Yes, there is a guarantee: "All things work together for good"—but only "for those who love God."

David and Solomon attained goodness and greatness because they had the wisdom to put first things first. Most of Judah's kings and all of Israel's lacked the wisdom of Solomon, who knew that "the fear of the Lord is the beginning of wisdom" (Proverbs 9:10). With a few notable exceptions (Joash, Josiah, the boy king, and Hezekiah), Solomon's successors did not understand that the true glory of Judah was her spiritual mission, her mission of mediation, her mission to bring men and women to God and God to men and women. They did not understand that apart from this mission as God's covenant people, the instrument of *God's* kingdom, *their* kingdom had no calling, no destiny, no distinctiveness, no purpose, no meaning, and no hope of greatness.

THE TEMPLE AND ITS LITURGY
FORESHADOW CHRIST

The significance of the temple is its messianic mission. Nothing in Scripture is significant apart from the Messiah, for nothing in the universe is significant apart from him (Colossians 1:15-20)! The significance of the temple was to foreshadow Christ's salvation in its liturgy, the Lamb of God with its ritual lambs, Easter with its Passover, and so on in each liturgical detail. Also the temple was to literally and physically receive the Messiah when he came.

Thus the temple foreshadows the liturgy of the Eucharist, which is that temple in which God continues to be really present with his people—a temple of flesh rather than of stone, but just as concrete. The tabernacles on our altars are not little images of the great Solomonic temple in Jerusalem; Solomon's temple is a mere image of the tabernacle that we know.

The climax and conclusion of *Chronicles* foreshadows the rebuilding of the temple in *Ezra* and *Nehemiah*. It is the decree of King Cyrus to allow the Jews to return home from their Babylonian captivity and rebuild their temple. (This Cyrus had been foretold by name by Isaiah the prophet [44:28; 45:1] apparently long before Cyrus was born.) *Chronicles* begins with Solomon building the original temple and ends with Cyrus authorizing its rebuilding four centuries later.

This "second temple" was destroyed by the Romans, together with virtually the entire city of Jerusalem in A.D. 70 and has never been rebuilt since then. One of the signs of the end of the world and the second coming of Christ according to some Christians, and of the (first) coming of the Messiah according to some Jews, is supposed to be the rebuilding of the temple. In light of this belief, even though it is not universally held, except among most Fundamentalist Christians, it is certainly an arresting fact that for the first time in nearly two thousand years some Jews are now openly speaking of plans to rebuild the temple, according to a recent story in *Time* magazine. Perhaps *Time* here unwittingly points to eternity.

In its fulfilled, Eucharistic sense, the temple has already been rebuilt. It is "rebuilt" thousands of times every day throughout the world. The symbol may or may not be rebuilt, but the reality it symbolizes is indestructible, for it is not an "it" but a "he," and he has promised, "Lo, I am with you always, to the close of the age" (Matthew 28:20).

TEN

God Brings Back His People to the Promised Land: Ezra and Nehemiah

*E*ZRA AND *NEHEMIAH* are companion books. They tell the story of the "second exodus," the return of the Jews to their homeland after seventy years of exile in Babylon.

There were three waves of deportation of the Jews to Babylon: in 606, 597, and 586 B.C. Then there were three waves of return. The first, in 538, was led by Zerubbabel; the second, in 457, was led by Ezra; and the third, in 444 B.C., was led by Nehemiah.

A MOMENTOUS TIME IN WORLD HISTORY

The period of time covered in *Ezra* and *Nehemiah* was crucial in world history. The philosopher Karl Jaspers calls it "the axial period" in the history of the world. About the same time the *Book of Ezra* was written (between 457 and 444 B.C.), Guatama Buddha lived in India (around 560-480 B.C.), Confucius (551-479 B.C.) and Lao Tzu (dates unknown) in China, and Socrates (470-399 B.C.) in Greece. All over the world at this time, great founders of spiritual traditions are calling their people to reconstitute their traditions on more inward and moral foundations. All over the world, spiritual history is turning a corner.

Yet only a small remnant of Jews returned from exile: a little less than fifty thousand out of the two or three million who were permitted to go. Imagine freeing three million prisoners and over 2,950,000 stay in their comfortable cells! During the first exodus, most of the Jews complained to Moses that life in Egypt had been more comfortable than the purgatorial wandering through the wilderness. We usually prefer comfort to freedom. Life in Babylon had been comparatively easy, but the trek to Jerusalem was nine hundred miles long (and there were no buses or trains!). Not only that, once they arrived, they faced a ruined land, city, and temple, along with the formidable task of rebuilding.

Those who returned were from the southern kingdom, the tribes of Judah, Benjamin, and Levi. The ten tribes of the northern kingdom are "the lost ten tribes of Israel." But a few representatives of these tribes probably returned as well; the "lost tribes" were not totally lost.

THE SECOND EXODUS UNDER KING CYRUS OF PERSIA

This second exodus took place when King Cyrus of Persia overthrew the Jews' conqueror, Babylon, and issued a decree freeing them to return home. A prophecy of this event appears in *Isaiah* (44:28-45:4), which even mentions Cyrus by name.

The return of many Jews from all over the world to the new homeland created for them again, for the first time in nineteen hundred years by the United Nations in 1948, has sometimes been called the third exodus. It has often been seen as a sign of the last days.

The second exodus was far less dramatic and impressive than the first exodus from Egypt. So too today's third exodus is less dramatic than Ezra's nine-hundred-mile trek from Babylon to rebuild the holy city and the temple.

Though Israel's days of glory seemed to be behind them in Ezra's time, and though this was true politically (the monarchy was never re-established), yet their true and greatest glory was still ahead of them. For their true glory was the spiritual glory (see Romans 3:1-2), which in the past had been their role as prophet to the world, especially as prophets of God's coming Messiah. Now in the future their greatest glory would be their role as the home and the people of God incarnate.

God's providential control over history and his care for his people are seen in his keeping his people safe even in exile. Both the second and the third exodus fulfill the promise made through Jeremiah (29:13-14):

> You will seek me and find me; when you seek me with all your heart, I will be found by you, says the LORD, and I will restore your fortunes and gather you from all the nations and all the places where I have driven you, says the LORD, and I will bring you back to the place from which I sent you into exile.

Christ is symbolized in *Ezra* in the same way he is in *Exodus.* As Moses is a Christ-symbol, leading God's chosen people out of captivity and Egypt (sin and worldliness) and to the promised land (heaven), so Ezra, Nehemiah, and Zerubbabel do the same. (Zerubbabel was also part of the direct Davidic messianic line: see 1 Chronicles 3:17-19 and Matthew 1:12-13.)

One reason why the Jews had to return from captivity was because in God's providential plan, Israel, not any other land, was to be the land of promise, that is, the land of the Messiah for Christians. The promised land does not mean merely the land God promised to give to the Jews for them to live in, but also the place God had prepared for the fulfillment of his supreme promise of salvation to the world. The Old Testament prophecies of the Messiah concerned Jerusalem and Bethlehem (Micah 5:2), not Babylon. The Messiah was not to be born in Babylon. *That* is the deeper reason why the Jews had to return.

THE PEOPLE REBUILD THE CITY WALL
AND BIND THEMSELVES TO THE LAW

The story of Ezra and Nehemiah is one of solidarity and recommitment in a time of trial. Ezra was a priest, in fact, a direct descendant of Aaron, the first high priest. He was also a scribe; thus he collected most of the books of the Old Testament. Tradition also ascribes to him Psalm 119, the longest psalm and the one in which the law is mentioned in every verse.

Nehemiah had been the cupbearer of Artaxerxes, king of Persia. (A cupbearer tasted the king's wine to prevent him from being poisoned.) This position meant that Nehemiah was a trusted official of the Persian court. He was allowed to leave Persia and lead the last group of Jews home from exile. (Ezra had already returned with the second group of exiles thirteen years earlier.)

Once home, Nehemiah challenged and organized the Jews to rebuild the wall of Jerusalem, for a city without a wall was hardly a city at all. It could be conquered easily. Like most saintly people, Nehemiah had to overcome opposition from his enemies and even from his friends. Yet the task was completed (the wall rebuilt) in only fifty-two days—a feat that so impressed Israel's enemies they knew God had to be on Israel's side.

Ezra and Nehemiah made up a team. While Nehemiah rebuilt the city wall, Ezra rebuilt his people's spirit. When he discovered that the people and even the priests had intermarried with Gentile women, he put a stop to this practice and led the people in repenting and recommitting themselves to the law. This separation from the other peoples was important because Israel had been chosen by God to be holy (the word means to be "set apart"), different from the world, to accomplish God's plan of salvation for the world.

Rebuilding the spiritual health of the people within the city wall was capped by the providential, nearly miraculous finding of a copy of the Scriptures, the *Book of the Law*. (The story of the preservation of all the books of the Bible makes one of the most amazing and exciting stories in literary history.) Nehemiah read this book to the people during a marathon, all day session, and the people wept with joy. (Contrast our reaction to an even slightly long Scripture reading at Mass!)

The reaction of the people to the reading of the law was to freely bind themselves to it, to their covenant with God. Now everything was restored except the king: the people were back, their commitment to be set apart as God's chosen people was restored, the covenant was restored, the Law was re-revealed, the city wall and the holy city of Jerusalem and its temple were all rebuilt. The kingly line was intact, but the true king who was to spring from that line, the Messiah, would not be a political ruler, as most of the Jews, even his own disciples, expected. (See the disciples' foolishly political question to him even after the resurrection in Acts 1:6.)

Nehemiah and Malachi, the last Old Testament prophet, lived at the same time, and both spoke against the same evils, especially cold-hearted indifference. There was to be over four hundred years between the time of Nehemiah and Malachi and the time of John the Baptist, Jesus' cousin and forerunner, who is the last prophet of the old covenant—four hundred years with no revelation from God. God used this period to prepare a hunger and an expectation in his people's hearts for the Christ to come. We can celebrate our easy Advent of four weeks because the Jews endured their hard Advent of four centuries.

ELEVEN

Biblical Heroines of Friendship and Courage: Ruth and Esther

THE BIBLE'S VIEW of women is not that of male chauvinism. Nor is it that of modern so-called "feminism," which is really an attack on all things feminine. Rather, without losing their feminine identity, heroines like Ruth and Esther and Deborah perform feats that the narrow-minded would restrict to men—much like St. Joan of Arc centuries later.

Ruth and Esther are the central characters of two little gems or short stories (short only in space, not in content), that are named after them. They come at two very different times: *Ruth*, before the era of kings, during the time of the judges; and *Esther*, after the era of kings, during the time of the exile. Both times are bad times, hard times. It is usually in such times that God raises up special saints.

Also these two women, in different ways, foreshadow the greatest woman and the greatest merely human being who ever lived, the Mother of God. They are thus appropriate subjects of reflection at Christmas since that season is the celebration of what Mary did in giving birth to Jesus, as much as it is the celebration of what Jesus did in being born from Mary.

RUTH: A WOMAN OF FAITHFULNESS
AND FRIENDSHIP

The inner beauty of the character of Ruth and the beauty of her story are like a gem shining against the dark background of sin, corruption, chaos, violence, and war during the time of the judges, before Israel chose its first king (Saul). It tells of some very ordinary people (the stuff saints are made of)—Ruth, Naomi, and Boaz—who remain faithful to God and to each other in faithless times and in a faithless nation. Once again, we are reminded of the truth of St. Thomas More's saying, "The times are never so bad that a good man cannot live in them."

The "good man" here is a woman. *Ruth* and *Esther*, along with *Judith* and *Susanna*, are the only books of the Bible in which a woman is the central character. Ruth is not a Jewish woman by birth or race, but a Moabite. The Moabites were descended from Lot, Abraham's nephew, not from Abraham. They were even less closely connected with the Jews than the Arabs, who are descendants of Abraham's son Ishmael. The Moabites worshiped not God but pagan idols, and were the military enemies of Israel, both before and after the time of Ruth. One of the lessons of this book, then, is universalism: God accepts Gentiles as well as Jews if they only believe in him. It is the same lesson as the one implied in the *Book of Jonah* and in the parable of the Good Samaritan.

All good stories with a happy ending must have an unhappy beginning. Ruth and Naomi begin in great misfortune: famine and the deaths of Naomi's husband and two sons. (Ruth was the widow of one of Naomi's sons.) Naomi probably thought God had abandoned her, but his providential plans surprise and surpass her expectations as they unfold in the events of the story (as they always do: cf. Ephesians 3:20; 1 Corinthians 2:9). They include a husband and a son for Ruth.

The name "Ruth" means friendship from the Hebrew

reuit. The story of Ruth is a story of friendship rewarded. Ruth's friendship with Naomi and with Naomi's God is the moving force behind the events of the story. This friendship and fidelity is expressed in the key verse, the most famous verse in the book (1:16). This is Ruth's choice to leave her pagan culture and religion and follow Naomi to Israel and to God: "where you go I will go, and where you lodge I will lodge; your people shall be my people, and your God my God." The choice for God brings reward as surely as the morning brings the light.

The reward in Ruth's case is not only her continued friendship with Naomi and escape from famine in Moab by accompanying Naomi to Israel, but also an unlooked-for love and happiness in meeting, loving, and marrying Boaz, and, even more, becoming the great-grandmother of David, Israel's greatest king, and through him the ancestor (the great-great-etc.-grandmother) of Christ himself, the Son of David and Son of God.

This family connection becomes especially significant when Boaz is factored into the equation. Boaz is a figure or symbol of Christ because he is the *goel*, or "kinsman-redeemer," the relative who saves Ruth from her state of widowhood and aloneness by redeeming her, buying her back to be his own, as prescribed by Jewish law. Christ did the same to all of us, of course. He too was our Redeemer, and also our kinsman, our relative. We are in his family physically for he is the Son of Man and mankind is one family through Adam.

It is said that no one on earth is more than seven steps removed from blood relationship to anyone else on earth. There have been only fifty-eight generations since Christ. Suppose you learned that you were the direct blood descendant of James, Christ's "brother" (i.e., cousin). But you are just as much a part of this same literal, blood family. Christ redeemed his whole family, human "kind." He can be our Redeemer only because he is the Son of Man (our kinsman) as well as Son of God.

In Jewish law, the *goel* had to be 1.) a blood relative of those he redeemed, 2.) free and in no need of redemption himself, 3.) *able* to redeem, and 4.) *willing* to pay the price to redeem. Boaz fulfilled all four requirements. So did Christ. In Boaz's case, the price of redemption was finite; in Christ's case, infinite: the very blood of God as the redemption of those of his blood relatives (humanity) who also choose to be his spiritual relatives, or adopted children, born "not of blood nor of the will of the flesh nor the will of man, but of God" (John 1:13).

Like Mary, Ruth was a kind of co-redeemer, for without her cooperation it could not have been done in this way. Ruth's bond "where you go, I will go. . . . Your God shall be my God" expresses the same state of soul, the same essential core of the spiritual life, the same secret of sanctity, as Mary's "fiat," "Be it done unto me according to thy word."

ESTHER: A COURAGEOUS WOMAN
SAVES HER PEOPLE

Here is another little gem of a book: a beautifully written story about a beautiful queen. Her name, "Esther," is Persian, and means "star." But she is a Jewess, in exile with her people in Susa, the great capital city of Persia. Her story is full of drama and suspense.

The evil Haman, a Jew-hater like Hitler, attempts genocide, just as Hitler did. Apparently, nothing can stop his plans, because he gets King Xerxes (Ahasuerus) to sign an edict to destroy the entire Jewish population in the whole Persian Empire, and any "law of the Medes and the Persians" that had been enacted by the king could never be changed. Such was Persian law. (For this reason, tradition says, the Persians would never enact a law unless they agreed on it twice: once while drunk and once while sober.)

The story tells how God raised up this Jewish girl to become the queen of the most powerful empire in the world in order to save his people from Haman and extinction. God uses ordinary people (Esther and her wise uncle Mordecai) to overcome apparently impossible obstacles to protect his people and keep his promises to Abraham many centuries before: "I will bless those who bless you, and him who curses you I will curse; and by you all the families of the earth shall bless themselves" (Genesis 12:3).

God's name is not mentioned even once in the original Hebrew version of this book (though it is in the later, Greek version, *"Second Esther,"* which is part of the Second Canon or Deuterocanonical books). But his providential hand is clearly seen by any attentive reader, just as it is in the long story of Joseph in Genesis 37-50. God's *supernatural* intervention is rare, whether in the form of verbal revelation or miraculous deeds; but God's providential control of the *natural* causes in history is omnipresent, and he is.

He works through human instruments and human wisdom, like Mordecai's, and even uses evil men, like Haman and Hitler, to contribute in the long run, against their own will, to his outcome; for he is the author of the story. He used even Satan in the *Book of Job* to fill a role in his plan, and also, more crucially, in the Gospels: even Judas turned out to be only a pawn in God's hands, which brought good ("Good Friday") out of evil.

In our own day, we can see how the modern Haman, Hitler, brought about *not* the extinction of the Jews, as he planned, by his holocaust, but the creation of the Jewish homeland, which, in the opinion of some historians, would not have happened without the Holocaust. Thus God can bring good even out of the worst of circumstances. Throughout history, God consistently blesses all who bless

Abraham's people, and destroys those who try to destroy them. For he blessed all people through this people by being born from them.

Read the exciting plot of this story yourself, and you will stand in awe of how thin was the thread on which God hung the survival of his people. For if Esther had not had the courage to face the Persian king and confess she was a Jew, and if Mordecai had not had the wisdom to escape Haman and counsel the king, there would have been no Christmas this year or any year.

TWELVE

Job Confronts Life's Darkest Problem and Encounters God Himself

I T IS UNIVERSALLY RECOGNIZED that *Job* is one of the greatest
books ever written, an all-time classic. It is terrifying,
beautiful, haunting, teasingly mysterious, tender, yet powerful as a sledgehammer—if only we read it with empathy and
openness and not try to "figure it out" as if it were a
detective story.

Though bottomlessly mysterious, its main point, or
lesson, is very obvious. It lies right on the surface, in the
words of God to Job at the end. Only a philosopher like
Rabbi Kushner, in his best-seller *When Bad Things Happen to
Good People,* can miss the message. If the problem of *Job* is the
problem of evil, then the answer is that *we do not know* the
answer. We identify with Job in his ignorance, not in his
knowledge.

The problem of evil, of suffering, of injustice in a world
ruled by an all-powerful and all-just God is life's darkest
problem. The reason why *Job* offers us no clear solution is
because the God of Job is not a philosophical formula, not a
bright, brittle little concept, but an infinite mystery. He is the

93

God Rabbi Abraham Heschel describes as "not an uncle, but an earthquake."

The dramatic interest in *Job* comes partly from the fact of the ironic contrast between Job's point of view and God's. The reader is allowed to share God's point of view too because of the preface (ch. 1), but Job is not. Thus there is a constant irony, a contrast between what seems to Job and what really is. God seems to be on trial; Job is really on trial. Job seems to be questioning God; God is really questioning Job.

THE LEVELS OF UNDERSTANDING JOB

Job is a many-layered book. Peel away surface layers and you find more underneath. Five of these layers are the following:

First, there is the problem of evil. How can a good God let bad things happen to good people? The solution of Job's three friends is simple: Job is not "good people." Faced with the apparent alternative between doubting God's goodness or Job's, they doubt Job's. It is a reasonable conclusion, but wrong, as we know from God's own words describing Job as "a sound and upright man, one who fears God and turns away from evil."

Second, there is the problem of the conflict between faith and experience. Job's faith tells him to expect just rewards; Job's experience shows him undeserved suffering. God's most important attribute in the Old Testament is probably his fidelity (*emeth*, "truth"), his trustability; and Job's experience seems to prove God untrustworthy. In fact, Job is on trial, not God, and he is proved trustworthy. God plays brinkmanship with him, but Job passes the test. As St. Paul says of God centuries later, he does not let us be tested beyond what we are able to endure.

Third, there is the problem of the meaning and purpose of

life, expressed in Job's question to God, "Why didst thou bring me forth from the womb?" (10:18). The question turns a different color when asked from agony. It is here not the philosopher's detached speculation but the sufferer's cry, "Why do you let this happen to me?" Job is like a small child's tear-stained face looking up at Daddy who has apparently let his child down.

Fourth, there is the problem of identity. When Job's three friends come to comfort him, they cannot recognize him at first (2:12), so disfigured he looks, sitting on his dung heap covered with sores. This is the Job who formerly sat in the city gates solving everyone's problems and shining forth as an example of justly rewarded righteousness. Has Job lost his identity? Just the opposite: his suffering brings him his deepest identity, as the sculptor's chisel strokes bring identity to a great statue.

Fifth, and deepest of all, there is the problem of God. Neither Job nor anyone in the Bible ever denies God's existence (except "the fool" in the Wisdom Books). But God's purposes and God's character and God's reliability are what is in question and what is revealed throughout the Bible and throughout *Job.* The question is not what God is in himself (the theologian's question) but who God is to me, to Job. This is the key to open the doors to solve the other problems as well, for it is God who gives Job his identity, his purpose, and his solutions.

Job's three friends are not fools. Readers often omit reading their speeches and concentrate only on Job, but this is a mistake. Their arguments are very strong. Their faith premise states that God is all-good and all-powerful, and rules his world with perfect justice. Their ethical premise adds that justice means rewarding the good and punishing the evil. Their common-sense premise further specifies that rewards are in the form of happiness and punishments in the form of misery, not vice versa. Their experiential premise is that Job is very miserable. Their logical conclusion is that

Job is very wicked. They do not argue in exactly that logical form, but with much more poetry and power, but that is the gist of their argument. Job cannot answer it.

A VISITATION FROM GOD HIMSELF

The answer the book suggests is first, that God's goodness and justice are far more mysterious than we think. Second, our blessedness is also far more mysterious. Long-range blessedness is purchased with short-range miseries. Suffering makes for wisdom, which is the heart of blessedness. That part of the solution is well known to all the sages.

What *Job* adds to the sages is that the essence of this long-range happiness is the vision of God himself, whom Job asked to meet face-to-face even if he must die. We must appreciate the Jews' deep fear of God and conviction that no one could see God's face and live, if we are to appreciate the drama of the ending of *Job*, where God shows Job his face and Job not only survives but is satisfied. For "I had heard of thee by the hearing of the ear, but now my eye sees thee" (42:5).

This ending answers another problem in *Job*: why is Job satisfied in the end, even though God does not answer a single one of Job's agonized and very good questions? Job is not a meek, humble, easily-satisfied man. He's from Missouri. George Rutler is right: we must not speak of the "patience of Job," but of the impatience of Job.

Job is satisfied by the only possible answer that would satisfy. If God had offered words, Job would surely have questioned those words again, and the verbal battle would have gone on eternally, as it does among our best philosophers. Instead of answers, Job got the answerer. Instead of words, Job got the Word. Job got the thing St. Thomas Aquinas asked for shortly before his death, when the Lord, speaking from the crucifix, said to him, "You have written well of me, Thomas; what will you have as a reward?" Thomas gave the world's best possible answer: "Only yourself, Lord."

Another problem is that of timing. Why does God hang Job out to dry for thirty-seven chapters? Why does Job have to go through his long and agonizing dark night of the soul? "Seek and you shall find"—but Job seeks and fails to find for a long time. Why?

GOD BECOMES THE QUESTIONER

Because God is the finder, not the found; the subject, not the object; the questioner, not the answer man; the initiator, not the responder. A God who would have showed up in response to Job's questions would not have been the true God, but a divine computer programmed to supply the answers if only we press the right buttons. When God does show up, the first thing he says is, "Now it is my turn to ask, and yours to answer." Just as Jesus hardly ever answers a question directly, but answers the questioner instead of the question, thus reversing the relationship and making the questioner the one who is challenged, so God reverses the roles in Job. Job learns that he is not asking God, "what is your meaning?" but God is asking Job "what is *your* meaning?" in and through the events of his life. It is true for all of us. Whenever we are led to ask, "What is the meaning of my life?" we are *being asked* exactly that question by God. We answer it not by words or thoughts only but by deeds, choices, and responses to life's challenges and sufferings.

Thus another problem is solved: *for whom* does God let Job suffer so? It certainly is not for the sake of the accuser, Satan, who is a mere instrument in God's hands, like a dentist's drill. Nor is it for God's sake, as if God were ignorant of the future and had to set up an experiment to find out whether Job would pass his test of fidelity.

So it must be for Job's sake. It must be out of God's love for Job. This would sound totally absurd to Job on the dung heap, of course, but it is perfectly understood by Job at the end, when he sees God face-to-face. God carved out a great hollow place for himself in Job with all these sufferings. Yet the hole made no sense until God came and filled it, as a lock makes no sense until the key comes.

SOLVING THE DEEP PUZZLE IN JOB 42:7

Finally, there is a deep puzzle in 42:7. God says that Job—who (by his own admission) uttered "wild words" of challenge to God, full of mistakes and even heresies (for example, that God is unjust)—spoke "rightly" about him, but that the three friends, who said nothing but pious orthodoxies, did not! But everything the friends say can be found in the rest of the Bible. How can this be wrong? Job contradicts it; how can this be right?

The friends spoke the truth, but not truly. Job spoke falsehoods, but truly. For the friends spoke *about* God as an absent, indifferent object, while Job spoke *to* God as a present, involved person. The three friends had a polite correspondence with God; Job had a stormy marriage with God, with fights but no divorce. The biggest difference between Job's speeches and those of the friends is that they only speak about God, while Job speaks to God. Prayer is the only accurate theology, for God is the I AM, not the IT IS. As Rabbi Martin Buber said, "God can only be addressed, not expressed."

Job is a Christ-figure. He is a "suffering servant," chosen by God to suffer not because he is so bad, but because he is so good. And he suffers for others. At the end, God accepts the three friends only because Job prays and sacrifices for them. In *Job* we see the Christological drama of death and resurrection played out not on the hill of Calvary outside the soul, but in a mirror image of it, a hole in the heart where the words "My God, my God, why hast thou forsaken me?" go up as a precious and redemptive offering to heaven. What happens in the *Book of Job* is the Mass, and Job is the altar.

THIRTEEN

Our Prayer Book
and Song Book:
The Psalms

THE BIBLE IS THE WORLD'S most popular book, but it is not one book but a whole library of books. In this library, *Psalms* is the most popular and most widely used book of the Bible. Thus *Psalms* is the most popular book in the world.

Psalms spans the ages. When we pray the *Psalms* we pray in union with David and the other ancestral composers of these prayers; in union with Christ and the apostles, who used them, as all Jews did and still do, as their favorite prayerbook and songbook; and in union with Jews and Christians in every age and place.

Psalms bridges the gap between Jews and Christians better than any other book can, for *Psalms* is not just Scripture, but also liturgy. Though Jews and Christians worship in different temples, they pray the same prayers to the same God. No theological cleverness, compromising, or negotiating is needed to bring us together: we are side by side as we pray these words.

Christians love the *Psalms* no less than Jews, from whom we inherited the book. But Christians add a messianic level of meaning to many of the psalms. A Christian sees Jesus' face in these words, as in the whole of the Jewish Scriptures. Yet this deeper, Christocentric level does not lessen or take away the other levels of meaning.

HOW THE PSALMS ARE MEANT TO BE USED

Psalms are songs as well as prayers. They are meant to be used, not just read. Prayer and singing are actions. The *Psalms* are more like instructions in a laboratory manual than like sentences in a textbook. We must perform them. They are more like sheet music than like a tape or record: we must play them on our own spiritual instruments.

Prayer was often *chanted* by ancient Jews and Christians, and still is by many peoples throughout the world. We should try this old "tried and true" method of praying by chanting, I think, both in private and in public, using either chants that are given to us or those we improvise ourselves. Even chanting a psalm in a monotone gives an effect that merely speaking it does not. Further, speaking it aloud gives an effect that reading it silently does not. It is like an echo; different walls of the soul add to the sound.

Most of us do not, and many of us can not, attend Mass daily. But everyone can pray a few psalms daily. And this is liturgy. Many of the psalms were and are used as part of the Jewish temple liturgy. The early church's liturgy was heavy with them, from the time of Christ and the apostles to the present day.

Today their role has shrunken, unfortunately, both in liturgy and in private devotions. In the liturgy, they are largely confined to the "responsorial psalm," which I think I have *never*, in attending about four thousand Masses, heard the congregation sing heartily. I think our liturgical "experts" have come up with the most unmelodic, unsingable, unmusical, and unmoving melodies for the *Psalms* in the history of music. This is a crime. We are being robbed of great riches and beauty by having these psalm gems surrounded by cheap settings, like putting diamonds in plastic.

The *Psalms* should be the foundation stone of every Christian's daily prayers. For to pray them regularly, to become familiar with them so that their phrases spring to mind spontaneously, is to shape our minds and hearts according to God's mind and heart. Here is the prayer book God himself inspired for us to use. Next to the "Our Father," they are the closest that human words will ever get to God's own answer to anyone who asks him, "Teach us to pray."

The *Psalms* were written from the widest possible range of feelings and situations, and *for* the widest possible range of feelings and situations. The *Psalms* are like the sabbath: "The sabbath was made for man, not man for the sabbath" (Mark 2:27). We find here a world as wide as we find in our own souls and lives: we find joy and despair, praise and complaint, certainty and doubt, defeat and success, suffering and liberation. We should become familiar enough with them to be able to go to the one that is appropriate to the present occasion and need. Or at least we should make a list or an index so that we know to use the one that fits. The locks of our hearts and lives are constantly changing, but the *Psalms* provide keys to fit all the locks. We just need to know where the keys are; we need to classify them. Simply "going through" them from beginning to end, while good, is not the best way to use them.

We will develop favorites, that we come back to dozens of times more often than we use other, less favorite ones. This too is good. It is like choosing personal friends.

Since the *Psalms* are poetry, the translation matters more here, I think, than in most of the books of the Bible. Our prayers need to be strong and clear and simple and intelligible. But they also need to be moving and beautiful. I heartily discourage the use of flat, pedestrian, colloquial translations like the one we've been using at Mass for ten or twenty years now.

In the original, the *Psalms* are stylized and poetic, not prosaic. The old Douay or King James versions were more accurate and more literal than most modern ones. The Revised Standard Version is a good blend of modern clarity and ancient beauty. So are many of the Jerusalem Bible's psalms, some of which were done by J.R.R. Tolkien, one of the great wordsmiths of the English language.

Though the *Psalms* span the range of a multitude of human attitudes, one stands out as their primary theme, the one they keep coming back to: praise, worship, adoration. If our prayers are not largely praise, they fail to conform to God's prayer pattern. Praise is our rehearsal for heavenly joy. Praise is tremendous therapy for self-absorbed, worried, and self-pitying souls, for praise is self-forgetful—one of the things we need the most. Praise looks at God, not at self. We praise God simply because he is God, because he is praiseworthy. Nothing else can free us from the terrible slavery to the thousand little tyrants of the modern world—our cares, worries, worldly responsibilities, and diversions—as well as self-forgetful praise of God. It need not be accompanied or motivated by *emotion;* merely *doing* it works healing within.

THE DIVISIONS IN THE PSALTER

The *Psalms* are divided into five books, each ending with a psalm of pure praise (41, 72, 89, 106, 150). They can also be divided into psalms for each of the four main purposes of prayer: 1.) adoration, 2.) thanksgiving, 3.) repentance, and 4.) petition. Or they can be further divided into:

1. psalms of praise (e.g., 18, 100, 103);
2. liturgical psalms (e.g., 120, 135);

3. psalms for pilgrimage, sung by pilgrims traveling up to Jerusalem (120-134 inclusive);
4. royal psalms, for the reign of the King of Kings (2, 20, 21, 28, 45, 72, 89, 101, 132, 144);
5. psalms of repentance (e.g., 32, 51, 130);
6. didactic, or moral teaching psalms (e.g., 1, 37, 119);
7. psalms for personal use (e.g., 23, 27, 34, 27);
8. cursing psalms (7, 35, 40, 55, 58, 59, 69, 79, 109); and
9. messianic psalms (e.g., 2, 22, 45, 110).

The cursing passages cannot, of course, be used by Christians unless we interpret them spiritually and remember that "for we are not contending against flesh and blood, but against the principalities, against the powers, against the world rulers of this present darkness, against the spiritual hosts of wickedness in the heavenly places" (Ephesians 6:12). We must hate sin, as these psalms and psalmists do; but we must not hate sinners, even if the psalmists did, failing to distinguish the two. Everything in Scripture is for our instruction, but not everything is for our imitation.

Many passages in the *Psalms,* as well as whole psalms, are messianic. If we had none of the rest of the Old Testament but only the *Psalms,* we would still be able to "check it out" and see that Christ fulfilled the Old Testament patterns and predictions. For instance, compare:

1. Psalm 2:7 with Matthew 3:17;
2. Psalm 8:6 with Hebrews 2:8;
3. Psalm 16:10 with Mark 16:6-7;
4. Psalm 22:1 with Matthew 27:46;
5. Psalm 22:7-8 with Luke 23:35;
6. Psalm 22:16 with John 20:25, 27;
7. Psalm 22:18 with Matthew 27:35-36;
8. Psalm 34:20 with John 19:32-36;
9. Psalm 35:11 with Mark 14:57;
10. Psalm 35:19 with John 15:25;
11. Psalm 40:7-8 with Hebrews 10:7;

12. Psalm 41:9 with Luke 22:47;
13. Psalm 45:6 with Hebrews 1:8;
14. Psalm 68:18 with Mark 16:19;
15. Psalm 69:9 with John 2:17;
16. Psalm 69:21 with Matthew 27:34;
17. Psalm 109:4 with Luke 23:34;
18. Psalm 109:8 with Acts 1:20;
19. Psalm 110:1 with Matthew 22:44;
20. Psalm 110:4 with Hebrews 5:6;
21. Psalm 118:22 with Matthew 21:42; and
22. Psalm 118:26 with Matthew 21:9.

(This list was compiled by Dr. Kenneth D. Boa.)

The *Psalms* are like an ocean fed by many rivers, many writers. They are for wading in, bathing in, swimming in, surfing in, boating on, and even drowning in (for the mystics have loved and used them too). Their authors include David (about half), Moses (90), Ezra (119), Solomon (72 and 127), Asaph, and many others. Psalm 90 is traditionally ascribed to Moses. They were written during a period of perhaps a thousand years, from the time of Moses, about 1400 B.C., to the return from exile, about 430 B.C.. They will last forever.

FOURTEEN

Our Road Map to Practical Wisdom: Proverbs

L ET US BEGIN WITH AN embarrassing problem about this book. Almost always, the more intelligent, clever, and original you are, the more bored you are by *Proverbs*. It tells you nothing you didn't know before. It is a book of platitudes, of old, well-worn truisms. It is, simply, dull.

Yes, that is how the most "advanced" minds see *Proverbs*. And our nation, our civilization, and our world are today threatened with destruction precisely because of the ideas of those "advanced" minds, because we have departed from the old platitudes. If there is anything our civilization needs in order to survive the threat of moral and spiritual and perhaps physical destruction, it is to return to these "safe," "dull" platitudes. For they are *true*. They are a road map to life, and we are lost in the woods.

That is what wisdom is: practical truth, truth for living, a road map. Another book of well-known practical wisdom very similar to Proverbs is the *Analects* of Confucius. The Western reader often finds them as tedious and uninteresting as *Proverbs*. Yet they were the blueprint for a society that lasted for two thousand one hundred years, arguably the world's most successful social experiment, at least in terms of longevity. Just as "you can't fool Mother Nature" ecologically, you also can't depart from nature's ways socially. The *Book of Proverbs* points out the two ways of life summarized by Psalm 1: the way that leads to life and health, and the way that leads to destruction. Even the most "advanced" and original minds cannot change that, for the maps come from God and from human nature itself, which he designed. Unless we somehow manage to be less bored by *Proverbs,* we will not be around much longer to be bored.

We are the first society in the history of the world that is losing its store of traditional proverbs. The older generation remembers hundreds; the younger generation, almost none. Every society in history has educated its young partly by proverbs. What is the significance of this fact? I think we can find at least four assumptions behind the use of proverbs that are so important that no society can survive without them.

THE VALUE OF PRACTICAL WISDOM

First, the assumption that practical wisdom is a real, true, objective thing, not just one man's "personal opinion." Consequently this thing, wisdom, is democratic rather than elitist, it is attainable by everyone, not just by the clever, the original, or the "experts."

Second, the assumption that most important things in life, which are the subjects of *Proverbs,* are knowable, are intelligible, at least partly. The great mysteries of life—life itself, and death, and good and evil, right and wrong, truth and falsehood, beauty, and joy, and human nature, and even God—are not opaque and hopeless holes of darkness but are meaningful and discoverable.

Third, that our lives here on earth are therefore meaning-ful, and patterned, something other than "vanity of van-ities" or "a tale told by an idiot, full of sound and fury, signifying nothing" except what we arbitrarily choose to make of them.

Fourth, that ordinary life experience is a more reliable teacher of this wisdom than university professors, newspapers, movies, or the boob tube.

Such beliefs are hopelessly old-fashioned today, of course. To return to them would be to turn back the clock. And that is exactly what we must do, for the clock is keeping very bad time indeed.

Like the *Psalms, Proverbs* is not meant to be read straight through as if it were a narrative. The book is a toolbench, a library: it is meant to be sampled, browsed through, picked at. It is a collection, assembled bit by bit and meant to be disassembled and used bit by bit. In our age of short attention spans, impatience, and only tiny slices of leisure time, it is an ideal book to dip into for a minute over your morning cup of coffee—much more useful than the morning paper. As Henry David Thoreau who despised newspapers used to say, "Read not the *Times;* read the eternities." These are the eternities.

Most of these proverbs were written by Solomon. Then a number of others, having learned from his example, added their own, sometimes anonymously. According to First Kings 4:32, Solomon wrote three thousand proverbs; this book includes some eight hundred of them. Solomon probably wrote them in his middle years, when he had progressed beyond youth enough to have acquired much wisdom from experience, but had not yet begun his decline into idolatry, folly, and immorality, which characterized his later years and which precipitated the catastrophic decline of the kingdom.

The reign of Solomon represented the one brief shining moment, the Camelot, of political Judaism. A proverb lies hidden in this historical situation, in fact, two: that the folly of one man can lead a whole people astray, and that the knowledge of three thousand proverbs is not enough to insure a good life: they must be practiced, not just preached (see Matthew 7:21-29).

According to Jewish tradition, Solomon wrote *Song of Songs* in his youth, *Proverbs* in his middle age, and *Ecclesiastes* in his old age. Most scholars doubt the Solomonic authorship of the other two books, though nothing is proven conclusively, but it is at least a fitting sequence symbolically. He journies from youthful idealism and beauty through the wisdom of maturity to the world-weariness and despair of an old man who had lost his spiritual youth. If he had only practiced his own proverbs, his old age would have been even more spiritually successful and blessed than his middle years.

THE LITERARY FORM AND THE KINDS OF WISDOM FOUND IN PROVERBS

Most of the proverbs have a literary form similar to that of the *Psalms:* parallelism through couplets. A short, pithy saying is first stated, then reinforced or (more often) contrasted with its opposite. The reason for this form is in the content, in the constant teaching of the "two ways" road map. The *Proverbs* are meant to be a guide to choosing the right way in a world full of sales pitches for the wrong way, a guide to living a good life in an evil world. Nostalgia buffs may long for the "good old days," but realists know that ever since Eden there are only the "bad old days." Every age is an evil age, that is why the warnings of the *Proverbs* are perennial.

Three different levels or kinds of wisdom can be distinguished in this book. First, some of the advice is purely practical and utilitarian: ways of prospering by the use of diligence, cleverness, prudence, and common sense. These are moral virtues too, but more obviously they are pragmatic virtues—means to the end of success. Second, there is the properly moral, ethical level, the extolling of righteousness and justice, charity and chastity, not only because they "pay off" but because they are right in themselves. Finally, the *Proverbs* also rise to the third and highest dimension of morality, where wisdom is seen as coming from God, streaming from God as sunbeams from the sun, made of the very stuff God is made of, a divine attribute, thus a way of being Godlike.

The first of these three levels is universal: every culture and every individual knows and lives by proverbs of pragmatic wisdom like "look before you leap." The second level is widespread but not universal. A small number of great ethical teachers like Plato rise to this level, and teach that "virtue is its own reward." But no one rose to the third level in the ancient world as well as the Hebrews, because the third level is the level of a moral relationship to God. The Hebrews had a special knowledge of and intimacy with God by a unique divine revelation. On this level, wisdom is more than practical prudence and more even than moral maturity and rightness of conduct in relating to others; it is "the fear of the Lord" (1:7; 3:5-6).

This "fear of the Lord" which is the beginning of wisdom is not, of course, a crude, cruel, or craven thing. It is high and holy and happy. It is the awe of adoration, the wonder of worship. Perhaps the main reason why the wisdom of the *Proverbs* is missing from the modern world is because its source, the fear of the Lord, is missing.

Even when we pay proper respect to God, we do not usually share or even sympathize with the "fear and trembling" that the ancients knew. Indeed, many of our modern "experts" in religious psychology, who write most of the textbooks, are convinced that their primary task is to wipe out that very thing. They regard as primitive and reactionary what divine revelation regards as the indispensable beginning of wisdom. We are free to choose which "expert" to follow in the matter of roads to God. But by the standards of even the lowest common denominator of prudential, practical wisdom, it would seem reasonable to let God tell us how to know God.

Probably the greatest and deepest passage in *Proverbs* is 8:22-31. The whole book merits endless rereading, but this passage especially rewards it. Here, wisdom, as a divine attribute, is personified (treated as a person). Usually personification is a mere literary device, a fiction. But in this case, it is not fiction but fact. For the wisdom of God *is* a person. He is the Second Person of the Blessed Trinity, who became a man in Jesus Christ. Even *Proverbs* is Christocentric. For it is Christ who "is the key that opens all the hidden treasures of God's wisdom," according to Colossians 2:3.

And just as *Proverbs* declares wisdom to be freely available to all (8:1-6, 32-35), so Christ is available to all. The clear and bold promise of the New Testament to any Christian is, "If any of you lacks wisdom, let him ask God, who gives to all men generously and without reproaching, and it will be given to him" (James 1:5). For we have already been given wisdom in having been given Christ. Wisdom is there. In fact, wisdom is not just *in* him, Wisdom *is* him: "God has brought you into union with Christ Jesus, and God has made Christ to be our wisdom" (1 Corinthians 1:30, TEV).

FIFTEEN

The Question the Rest of the Bible Answers: Ecclesiastes

THIS BOOK IS UNIQUE among all the books of the Bible. It is the Bible's only book of philosophy. Philosophy is the wisdom of human reason alone, without any appeal to divine revelation. In this book God is silent. In the rest of the Bible, God speaks.

In *Job*, for instance, we have a similar book, about a similar philosophical problem, the problem of an apparently meaningless and empty life. But in *Job*, God speaks to Job. In *Ecclesiastes*, Ecclesiastes only speaks to God. Not even that; he only speaks *about* God. The method the author uses is the scientific method: sense observation of the visible appearances of life "under the sun," plus human reasoning about it.

This book is the question to which the rest of the Bible is the answer. Whatever rabbis originally decided to include it in the canon of sacred Scripture were wise and courageous, for the question it poses is a deep and challenging one. Only great confidence in the even deeper answer they had in the rest of the Bible must have prompted them to approve this deep, dangerous question. It is dangerous because if there is no adequate answer to it, we are left with the world's worst bad news without the good news, without a gospel. For the thing we need most of all, meaning and purpose and hope, "a reason to live and a reason to die," is precisely the thing questioned and doubted in this book.

The last six verses (12:9-14) were probably added by a second author, who answered the first one by summarizing the answer of Judaism and the rest of the Old Testament: "The end of the matter; all has been heard. Fear God, and keep his commandments; for this is the whole duty of man." This positive answer contrasts sharply with the negative lack of answer to the question of life's meaning that the rest of the book begins and ends with: "Vanity of vanities, all is vanity."

No one knows who authored the book. He called himself "the Preacher ('Ecclesiastes'), the son of David (Solomon), king in Jerusalem" (1:1), but this was a common literary device of authors of "wisdom" for many centuries after Solomon. It is as if a philosopher today would use the pen name "Socrates," meaning "a disciple of Socrates."

THE CENTRAL MESSAGE OF ECCLESIASTES

The main point of the book is so obvious that it is stated five times at the beginning (1:2), then three more times at the end (12:8). It is "vanity." "Vanity" means, of course, not the absence of humility, as in a "vanity mirror" but the absence of meaning and purpose, as in a "vain search." The book's structure mirrors its content: it is circular, it goes nowhere, it ends on precisely the same note it began with: "Vanity of vanities, all is vanity."

The author tells how he tried at least five different lifestyles, five candidates for the position of life's meaning, five keys to unlock the strange hollow door of life, and how he found each one of them inadequate. He tried wisdom (1:12-18); pleasure (2:1-11); wealth and power (2:8); honor, prestige, or working for posterity (2:18-19); and a conventional, legalistic, external religion (7:16-18). Each one failed because it was only a this-worldly key, and life has an other-worldly door. It was only a finite peg, and the human heart has an infinite hole. It was only a little answer, and he was asking a very big question. Even his God is not an adequate answer because his God is a mere object, like the moon. He is *there*, but he is not *here*. He makes no difference. He is an ingredient in the cosmos, a piece of furniture in life's stage set, and not the Lover and Savior that he really is.

Along the way of ultimate despair, little hopes and little wisdoms emerge from the darkness. There is a lot of good practical advice scattered throughout this book like oases in a desert. But the main thrust is the desert, the emptiness, the vanity.

Ecclesiastes lays bare the God-sized hole in the human heart that all God-substitutes fail to fill—the emptiness left by the removal of God to a position of remoteness and irrelevance. This is the very emptiness that modern men and women have covered up by the thousand distractions of the most detailed, diverting, and demanding civilization in history. *Ecclesiastes* blows our cover. Infinitely superior to the bland blandishments of pop psychology with its shallow ideals of feel-good rather than be-good, *Ecclesiastes* rises to the dignity of despair.

THE FIVE REASONS FOR VANITY

The five lifestyles or values that Ecclesiastes tries are precisely the five tried in all ages and cultures, from ancient Hinduism's "Four Wants of Man" through Augustine's *Confessions* to modern existentialist novels like Sartre's *Nausea* and Hesse's *Siddhartha*.

Ecclesiastes finds that no matter which way he turns, all of his life is surrounded by five features which make for vanity, five reasons for his ultimate conclusion. First, a blind fate seems to rule life, so that nothing makes any difference. Neither wisdom nor foolishness, neither good nor evil really matter in the end (2:13-17; 9:2-3).

Second, it all goes down the drain in death anyway, it seems, and he sees nothing beyond death (3:19-21; 9:4-6). Clear revelation of life after death did not come until quite late in the history of God's revelation.

Third, life is full of evil and injustice (3:16; 4:1-3; 10:1).

Fourth, time seems to be a cycle that goes nowhere, a merry-go-round without the merry. Everything returns again. There is no ultimate progress, no hope, no gain, "nothing new under the sun" (1:4-11; 3:1-9). If you take your philosophy of time from the cycles of nature rather than from the growth of the soul, then that is indeed what time looks like.

Finally, even God seems to be part of the problem rather than part of the solution, for without faith and divine revelation, mere human experience and reason cannot understand God and his ways. His purposes remain hidden and unknowable (7:13; 8:17; 11:5).

THE RELEVANCE OF ECCLESIASTES TO TODAY

It is impossible to overemphasize the importance of the question, the challenge, posed by *Ecclesiastes*, especially for our age. The book is quintessentially modern in at least five ways. It asks the modern *question:* does life have any ultimate meaning? It assumes the same modern *context,* in which religion is reduced to observed behavior and conventional observance. It uses the modern scientific *method* of sense observation, taking accurate pictures of life with the available light of reason, but no faith flashbulb added to the camera. It comes to the modern *conclusion* of vanity, nothingness, and "the existential vacuum." It even concludes with the modern *practical advice* of hedonism, "seize the day," "eat, drink, and be merry, for tomorrow we die." But there is always the grinning skull lurking behind the parties (9:7-10).

It is absolutely essential that we answer *Ecclesiastes'* question and challenge. If we do not, we have no reason, ultimately, to do anything else, anything at all. The argument can be summarized in a single logical syllogism:

All of life ("toil") takes place in the world
  ("under the sun");
And everything in the world ("under the sun") is
  ultimately "vanity";
Therefore all of life is ultimately vanity.

There are only three ways to answer any argument: to find a term the argument has used ambiguously; or to find a logical mistake or fallacy in the argument; or to find a false premise or assumption. We cannot do the first or second things, but we can do the third. In fact, in light of the rest of the Bible, *both* premises are false!

First, there is a "toil" that is not "under the sun," a human work that is not confined to this world: the building of the kingdom of heaven. "Only one life, 'twill soon be past; only what's done for Christ will last." What we are doing here is not just filling our stomachs and our bank accounts, but building the mystical body of Christ, the kingdom of loving souls. If our souls are redeemed, our bodies and even our world will also be redeemed in the Resurrection of the Dead. Death is not a hole, but a door; not the end, but the beginning.

Second, there is one thing here "under the sun" that escapes "vanity." There is a sixth key that Ecclesiastes never tried, but the author of the next book in the Bible tried. It is love. Love is the meaning of life because love is the very nature of the God who designed life. In other words, Ecclesiastes' fifth key, conventional religion, is a counterfeit. True religion is the love of God and neighbor. Try that; you'll like it.

Even though we have argued against Ecclesiastes and answered his challenge as an opponent, this book is tremendously valuable for us, though it begins and ends in despair. For it exposes the God-shaped hole in the human heart with tremendous honesty. As St. Augustine said, "Thou hast made us for thyself, and [therefore] our hearts are restless until they rest in thee."

Ecclesiastes did not realize the first half of Augustine's saying, but he certainly realized the second half. Like modern man, he tried to quiet his restless heart in vain, trying to fill an infinite hole with finite pegs. It is like trying to fill the Grand Canyon with marbles. Nothing is big enough to fill the emptiness, nothing is stronger than death and evil—except one thing. That one "thing" is a Person. Christ came to conquer death and evil. Ecclesiastes highlights the problem; Christ is the answer. All of the Bible points to him in one way or another.

SIXTEEN

The Great Love Story between God and the Soul: Song of Songs

THIS BOOK HAS BEEN the favorite of great saints, yet it is the only book of the Bible that never once mentions the name of God. Why? Because God is everywhere in this book, symbolically. The bridegroom, Solomon, stands for God; and his lady fair, his chosen bride, stands for the soul or the church, the New Israel. The book has traditionally been interpreted on two levels: literally, as a celebration of married love, and symbolically, as a celebration of the joys of our spiritual marriage to God.

The symbolic interpretation is consistent with the rest of Scripture, which sees Israel, both the old and the new, as God's bride: Isaiah 54:5-6; Jeremiah 2:2; Ezekiel 16:8-14; Hosea 2:16-20; 2 Corinthians 11:2; Ephesians 5:23-25; Revelation 19:7-9; 21:9-10. The symbolic interpretation does not replace the literal. God designed sexual love in marriage to be one of life's greatest joys, and to reflect the one-in-many-ness of God (Genesis 1:27-28; 2:24). It is fitting that the most complete and intimate human relationship is used as God's chosen symbol for the even more intimate marriage between God and the loving soul.

Love is the very nature of God (1 John 3:8). Therefore it is the ultimate reason for everything God does, everything in the story of our lives, the story he designs. Life is a love story, behind the appearances of a tragedy, a war story, a detective story, or a mishmash. This book implicitly answers the great question: What is the ultimate meaning of life? What kind of a story are we in? What is the answer to Ecclesiastes' "vanity of vanities"? The answer to all three questions is love. This book lifts the curtain of God's providence, and lets us see behind it into the mind of the author and director backstage.

All four loves are present here: *eros* or desire (8:5); *storge* or affection (4:9); *philia* or friendship (5:16); and *agape* or charity (2:16). This is because married love is the most complete of loves. Husband and wife give their whole selves to each other (2:16). That is why the church opposes contraception: something is held back. The natural end and purpose of married love is to join the unitive and procreative, to ensure the psychological and biological completeness of the union. Contraception breaks this unity, this divine design.

Song of Songs is a dramatic series of love poems. It is a dialog—like life itself, which is a dialog between God and the soul, mediated by everything in the universe. Poems do not preach, but they show. Here are some of the things this poem shows about love, both human and divine.

SOME OF THE IMPORTANT TRUTHS ABOUT LOVE

1. Love is a song, according to the title. Music is the natural language of love, more profound than words. We do not speak of love *speeches*, but of love *songs*. Song is not ornamented speech; speech is song made prosaic. God sang creation into being because God is love.

2. Love is the greatest song, the "song of songs" in Hebrew idiom, the song that includes all songs. All events

that ever happened are notes in this song. It is also greatest in value (8:7); nothing can buy love.

3. Love is a perpetual motion machine. The more the groom loves the bride, the more the bride loves the groom, and vice versa, without end. This is why heaven will never be boring or static. Each singer "caps" the other's line (1:15-17; 2:2-3).

4. Love is not sweetly swoony and sleepy, but bright and energetic, like the images of sun, moon, morning, and a bannered army (6:10). Love is news, good news, gospel, ever-young, hopeful, and promising (2:10-13).

5. Love is also work (3:1-4), hard work. Sheldon Vanauken, author of the magnificent, moving autobiographical love story *A Severe Mercy*, says the most frequent question he is asked is how he and his wife managed to have such a real love story that everyone else envies and almost no one else attains. His simple answer: We worked at it.

6. Love is perfected by suffering. In turn, it perfects suffering. At first, the consummation of their love is only yearned for (1:2; 2:6). But after the bride suffers in the wilderness (1:5-6; 8:5), then there is trust: "Who is that coming up from the wilderness leaning upon her beloved?" Before that, he had to cajole her from hiding: "O my dove, in the clefts of the rock, in the covert of the cliff, let me see your face, let me hear your voice, for your voice is sweet, and your face is comely" (2:14). God purifies the soul by suffering and hollows out a place for himself. In suffering we hear the whispers of divine love. In turn, love consecrates suffering and turns it into a spiritual marriage bed (8:5).

7. Love is free, and cannot be compelled, even by omnipotence. The bride asks the groom to "draw me after you" (1:4), not to pull, push, or carry her. The one thing even God cannot do is force us to love him. How much less can we force each other. God will seduce our souls, but he will not rape them. Love and force are contradictories. Thus the

groom repeatedly cautions us, "I adjure you, O daughters of Jerusalem [audience], that you stir not up nor awaken love until it please" (2:7; 8:4).

8. Love is not blind. Love is the most perfect accuracy. How could love be blind?—God is love. Is God blind? "Rightly do they love you" (1:4). Only the eyes of love perceive the truth of the beloved's loveableness. Who knows you better, your simple friend who cares deeply about you, or your brilliant acquaintance who knows more about you but loves you less?

Yet the symbolic interpretation of the poem is severely tested since the groom (God) says such amazing things about the bride (our sinful souls) that he seems blind indeed: "You are all fair, my love; there is no flaw in you" (4:7). How can this be? It can be because God speaks from eternity, from heaven, where we will indeed be flawless. It is prophecy. It is destiny. It is the biologist knowing the caterpillar and seeing therein the butterfly. Dante apparently shared something of this heavenly vision of Beatrice, and he insisted that the vision was objectively true and accurate. For what God sees cannot be inaccurate. If God tells you, as he does here, that you are so beautiful that he can hardly bear to look at you (4:9; 6:5), you'd better rethink your self-image, for you are made in the image of King God, not King Kong.

9. Love is as simple and perfect as the poetry that expresses it (see 1:15-17). Nothing fancy is needed: no additions, subtractions, distractions, or complications. Love is simple because God is simple. (It is also infinitely mysterious.)

10. Love is individual. "As a lily among brambles, so is my love among maidens" (2:2-3; 5:9-10; 6:8-9). The object of true, divine love is not "humanity" (if preachers tell you that, they're preaching a different gospel from Jesus' gospel) but "neighbor," the concrete, unique individual. You can only ever love individuals, because only individuals ever exist. Classes and collections are abstract objects of thought, not

concretely real things. We group people into groups, but real people are concrete individuals.

11. Love is all-conquering (2:8). *Amor vincit omnia*, "love conquers all." Obstacles are flattened: "Every mountain and hill shall be made low." Love leaps over obstacles like a gazelle. Nothing stops love.

12. Not even death can conquer love. Love is "strong as death" (8:6). Its fire cannot be drowned by death's waters (8:7). For God is love, and God conquered death for us. When your beloved's body dies, the love between you does not die, because love is between immortal souls.

13. Love is surprising (2:8-9; 5:2), not planned. It is like God: he never comes in the expected time or way. He is bigger than our expectations. Therefore the only way to control and master our lives is to keep love out. Love's wind reshuffles our house of cards over and over again.

14. Love casts out fear (2:14; cf. 1 John 4:18). That is why Jesus is always saying, "Fear not." We all have fear, especially those who scorn it most. And nothing but love, no bluff, no substitute, will cast it out.

15. Love somehow mysteriously exchanges selves (2:16). I am not mine but yours; you are not yours but mine. And this is the only way for me to be truly me and you you. The gift given in love is more than feelings, deeds, time, or even life: it is the very self. The very giver becomes its own gift.

16. Love is glorious, triumphalistic, a twenty-one-gun salute, a fireworks display (3:7-11). Thus the military imagery—the loud, colorful, verbally shouting style of Scripture. How different from the "nice," wimpy, weepy, weary, and weak worldly loves that our "sharing and caring" gurus patronize us with!

17. Love is natural. Therefore it uses countless nature images. Everything in nature is an analogy or a symbol for this supreme point of all creation (see 4:1-5; 5:11-15; 7:2-9). Love fulfills nature as well as humanity.

18. Love is faithful and monogamous (4:12; 8:6). Love is

already free, so it does not long to be free but to be bound forever. That is not its servitude, but its joy and fulfillment.

19. Love is ready, like Mary's "fiat." In the poem, the bride is not ready for the groom (in 5:2-8), and suffers terribly because of it. When God's love calls, we must respond immediately. (The word "ready" is constantly used of Jesus' actions in Mark's Gospel.)

There is much more in the poem than these few suggestions, and even more in the greater poem that is life itself lived in love with God and each other. But these should suffice to "prime the pump." The way to read a poem like this is with the unconscious, intuitive mind freely imagining and associating. This greatest of love poems has been a bottomless well of wisdom and joy to saints like Bernard, John of the Cross, and Thomas Aquinas. If it nourished their great souls, it can certainly nourish our little ones. There is one "trick," however: only a lover can understand it. The way to comprehend it is to do it. "If your will were to do the will of my Father, you would understand my teaching" (John 7:17).

SEVENTEEN

God's Big Mouths: The Prophets

W HY DIDN'T ISRAEL have an excess prophets' tax? Are there still prophets today? How can we tell a true prophet from a false one? Why did St. Paul call prophecy the most important of all spiritual gifts? How can we read the prophetic books of the Old Testament without getting bogged down? These chapters on the biblical prophets will try to answer such questions.

To begin at the beginning, just what *is* a prophet? The word in Hebrew means literally "mouth." A prophet is God's mouthpiece. It is an Old Testament foreshadowing of the New Testament idea that we are organs in the Body of Christ, God's hands and feet on earth. Prophets are the Body's mouth. A great prophet is a big mouth.

Big mouths are what they were, and they all got in trouble for it. A prophet tells too much truth to be socially approved. A "popular prophet" is a contradiction in terms. Just being unpopular doesn't make you a prophet, but just being a prophet does make you unpopular. The greatest prophet of all (who was more, but not less, than a prophet) said this to his disciples: "Woe to you, when all men speak well of you, for so their fathers did to the false prophets" (Luke 6:26).

Being a prophet means sharing in the holy unpopularity of the Lord of all the prophets: "A servant is not greater than his master. If they persecuted me, they will persecute you" (John 15:20). The job description for prophet has few perks. Indeed, the only one of all the Old Testament prophets who volunteered was Isaiah (6:8). All the rest were drafted, dragooned.

But though there's no earthly profit in being a prophet, there is an earthly need. If the prophet's intended audience already knew or liked the prophet's message, the prophet would be superfluous. Prophets must tell us what we do *not* know or want to know.

THE ESSENTIAL FUNCTION OF A PROPHET

Prophets are the spiritual FAX machines God uses to get his message through. Prophets are like miracles that way: signs of the supernatural. The Greek word for "miracle" means literally "sign."

Try to imagine how God could get his infallible truth through to our fallible minds without supernatural intervention—miracles and prophets. How could we know which of our human ideas had the divine approval without prophets as touchstones? The liberal or modernist interpretation of prophets, which subtracts the miraculous or supernatural, subtracts precisely the essential function of the prophet, the function of touchstone.

We need not be fundamentalists to be orthodox, but we must be supernaturalists. We need not think God dictated to the prophets word for word, but we must believe the prophets' words are divinely, not just humanly, inspired.

But, the modernist might counter, many people claim divine inspiration and say, "Thus says the Lord!" If there are true, God-given prophets, how could we tell them from false, merely human ones?

The Bible gives two very simple answers to that question. One comes from Jesus: "By their fruits you shall know them" (Matthew 7:16). The other comes from Moses, the greatest Old Testament prophet, who spoke with God face-to-face. When Moses was about to die and the Jews were about to enter the promised land, Moses knew there would be false prophets as well as true ones, and that the Jews needed a simple rule for discernment. The rule is simply: wait. The word of the true prophet will always come true.

It is not the only function of a prophet to foretell. He is more a forthteller than a foreteller, but he is a foreteller too. All merely human foretellers will err. Only God is eternal and knows our future as his present. God's mouth never errs. God's mouthpieces will have a batting average of 1.000; false prophets will always bat under 1.000 and over .000. (A prophet whose predictions were always false would be as infallible and as useful as one whose predictions were always true. There are bound to be some good guesses among the Nostrodamuses or the Jean Dixons.)

God's promises are true because they *come* true in time, in history. To see the truth, we need only patience and the long view of things—like the classicist who waits for time to reveal a true classic.

It's worth waiting for. St. Paul ranks prophecy first among all the spiritual gifts (1 Corinthians 12:31; 14:1). Why? Because it "edifies," it builds the church. The Word of God, and the will of God expressed in the Word of God, is the very food of the church. No body can grow, can be built up, without food. To know and do God's mind and will is our real food (John 4:34; 6:55).

THE PROPHET TELLS US GOD'S MIND

There are three essential steps in the process of "edification": knowing God's mind, doing God's will, and sharing

God's life. The prophet starts the process by telling us God's mind, especially when ours has run off the track. We can't attain our ultimate destiny, sharing God's life, without doing God's will. But we can't do it unless we know it.

That is why prophets are so important: they are a lifeline to God. It's not just a matter of information or curiosity, but a matter of life or death to know "Thus says the Lord."

In Old Testament Judaism there were three crucial tasks, and three kinds of leaders: prophets, priests, and kings. (Jesus culminated and fulfilled all three.) Every society needs some form of these three, as a ship needs a navigator (who is like a prophet or a seer), a first mate (who is like a priest, interceding between the captain and the crew), and a captain (who is like a king).

Most great works of literature have three characters for these three functions. *The Lord of the Rings* has Gandalf, Frodo, and Aragorn. *The Brothers Karamazov* has Ivan, Alyosha, and Dmitri. "Star Trek" has Mr. Spock, Dr. McCoy, and Captain Kirk. Even Jesus' disciples had an "inner circle" of John, James, and Peter.

The reason can be seen in the very structure of the human soul. Plato first formulated this three-part structure as intellect, desires, and "the spirited part." Freud called them the super-ego, id, and ego. Common sense calls them mind, feelings, and will. These are our interior prophet, priest, and king.

UNDERSTANDING AND READING THE PROPHETS

The books of prophecy in the Old Testament contain the writings of only the later Hebrew prophets. The earlier prophets wrote either historical books (Moses, Samuel) or no books (Elijah, Elisha). There are 16 prophetic books, divided into four "major prophets" (*Isaiah, Jeremiah, Ezekiel,* and *Daniel*) and twelve "minor" ones. The four "major" prophets wrote longer, more profound, more exalted, or more wide-ranging books.

There is a "trick" to reading these books. We can't expect just to plow through them as we would plow through a story. We should know the background stories, the historical settings, and problems in which the prophets worked. So the books of the prophets should be read in conjunction with the historical books.

Also we must not try to read their poetry as prose. This is more than just a question of interpreting correctly, a question of symbolic versus literal meaning. Sometimes poetry can be very literal. Rather, it is a question of attitude. When we read poetry we must take a different attitude toward words. In prose, words are our instruments, our servants. In poetry, they are our masters. To understand poetry we must stand under it. Its words are not tools, but jewels. We must hoist them, dangle them, admire them, and let the light play with them.

The right way to interpret prophetic poetry is *midrash*, the traditional Jewish method which is itself poetic, personal, intuitive, and even mystical, rather than scientific and scholarly. *Midrash* reads with the heart as well as the mind; in awe, not curiosity. For this is *God* who speaks! To hear God, we need more than the functions of ear and mind, we need the prefunctional root, the heart. Solomon says, "Keep your heart with all vigilance, for from it flow the springs of life" (Proverbs 4:23). Only one whose heart is open to God's heart will understand God's prophets (see John 7:17).

The prophets' verbal gems, like diamonds, were hammered out under great pressure. Prophets appear during times of crisis, spiritual emergency, sin, and decay. Times like ours.

But are there prophets today? Indeed there are, though not canonical ones, for the canon is closed, the "deposit of faith" completed. Today prophets water the trees God planted in Scripture. The gift of prophecy, confined to a small number in Old Testament times, is spread to the whole church.

Who are today's prophets? Individual popes and saints to be sure, but above all the church itself, which Christ left as a permanent prophet and "sign" for the whole world. One mark of her true character as prophet is her unpopularity. Like her Lord she draws down the wrath of the world and its media upon herself when she dares to speak the whole truth entrusted to her instead of editing or abbreviating it. G.K. Chesterton said, "I don't want a church that tells me when I'm right; I want a church that tells me when I'm wrong." But not many are as wise as Chesterton. Why should the world love the church? Does a cavity love a dentist?

But true prophets were never merely negative. The one-word summary of their message—"repent"—has two sides. "Repent" means "turn," and there is both a turning-from and a turning-to. The first is only there for the second.

All the prophets show us two ways: the way of life and the way of death (see Psalm 1). Thus "a prophet of doom" is a contradiction in terms, for all prophets are prophets not of doom but of free choice. Moses sums up all subsequent prophets' message this way: "I call heaven and earth to witness against you this day, that I have set before you life and death, blessing and curse; therefore choose life, that you and your descendants may live, loving the LORD your God, obeying his voice, and cleaving to him; for that means life to you" (Deuteronomy 30:19-20).

There are always two ways; and they end in two places just as real, and as different, as the ends of two physical roads. The prophets give us road maps, well marked with signs. We must do the choosing and the traveling.

Most important of all, the true way the prophets point us to is not an abstract "lifestyle," but the Person who said, "I AM the Way, the Truth, and the Life."

EIGHTEEN

The Shakespeare of Prophecy Thunders with the Message of Salvation: Isaiah

HEBREW NAMES ARE MORE THAN LABELS. They tell the identity, the significance, the sign-value of the person who bears them.

The name "Isaiah" means "God is salvation." That's the bottom line of Isaiah's prophecies. His book has been called "the Gospel according to Isaiah," for his prophecies of the Savior are more numerous, beautiful, and famous than those of any other prophet.

Isaiah has been called "the Shakespeare of the prophets," for his poetry is the strongest and most exalted among them. Only *Job* and *Psalms* rival *Isaiah* in the whole Bible, perhaps in the whole of human literature, for poetic grandeur.

At least ten passages of *Isaiah* have become unforgettable to all English-speaking peoples because of Handel's use of them in the world's favorite oratorio, "The Messiah": 11:1-5; 7:14; 40:9; 60:2-3; 9:2; 9:6; 35:5-6; 40:11; 53:3-6; 53:8.

Whenever we hear these verses read, we hear Handel's

music. It doesn't take an effort to join these texts and the music; it takes an effort to separate them now. I expect to hear them in heaven.

Before reading the rest of *Isaiah,* you should begin with chapter 6, the story of God's call to Isaiah to be his prophet: "And I heard the voice of the Lord saying, 'Whom shall I send, and who will go for us?' Then I said, 'Here am I! Send me.' And He said, 'Go, . . .' "

The awesome simplicity of the language reflects the awesome simplicity of the experience, which in turn reflects the awesome simplicity of God.

If anyone thinks that linguistic style is a mere dispensable ornament added to the "message," and that therefore a business-report-style translation is as good as a poetic one, let him read the following passage from Isaiah 6 in its old, rich, poetic, *and literal* translation (Revised Standard Version, an excellent literal translation) and then compare a prosaic modernization:

In the year that King Uzziah died I saw the Lord sitting upon a throne, high and lifted up; and his train filled the temple. Above him stood the seraphim; each had six wings: with two he covered his face, and with two he covered his feet, and with two he flew. And one called to another and said: "Holy, holy, holy is the LORD of hosts; the whole earth is full of his glory." And the foundations of the thresholds shook at the voice of him who called, and the house was filled with smoke. And I said: "Woe is me! For I am lost; for I am a man of unclean lips, and I dwell in the midst of a people of unclean lips; for my eyes have seen the King, the LORD of hosts!"

(Hardly a passage likely to be selected by one of those modern religious educators who's been taught that the beginning of wisdom is to eradicate that horrible, crude thing called "the fear of the Lord"—which the Lord's own

Word calls the beginning of wisdom: Job 28:28; Proverbs 9:10.)

Now compare a modern translation:

Each creature covered its face with two wings, and its body with two, and used the other two for flying. They were calling out to each other: "Holy, holy, holy! The Lord Almighty is holy. His glory fills the world" . . . I said, "There is no hope for me!"

Make the same comparisons with the ten passages from Handel's "Messiah" listed above, and send your results to the International Commission on English in the Liturgy (ICEL), please.

I used to think the old, poetic versions of the Bible were "jazzed up" and that the newer versions were more literal. Then I found that it was exactly the opposite: The new translations take out the high poetic style that is in the original, while the old translations were literal and left it in. Imagine my surprise, my joy (about the real, literal translators), and my anger (at the robber-translators).

ISAIAH: A SUMMARY OF THE OLD AND NEW TESTAMENT

The *Book of Isaiah* is like a diptych, a two-panel altarpiece. The first panel paints a picture of God's justice and judgment; the second panel, of God's mercy and forgiveness. By a neat little trick of divine providence, the first panel consists of thirty-nine chapters, the same as the number of books in the first canon of the Old Testament (not counting the Deuterocanonical Books); and the second panel consists of twenty-seven chapters, the same as the number of books in the New Testament.

The first panel is a summary of the Old Testament's message—judgment, justice, and the need for repentance—

and the second is a summary of the New Testament's message of salvation, mercy, and the need for faith and hope. These two truths have always been the two central truths of every orthodox Christian theology, from St. Paul's *Epistle to the Romans* through Augustine's *Confessions* to Pascal's *Pensees:* the Bad News and the Good News, problem and solution. These are the two things we most need to know, the two words that summarize Jesus' preaching: repent and believe. *Isaiah* is the whole Gospel in theological miniature and poetic magnification.

Like the Savior he foretold, Isaiah was tortured and murdered, according to Jewish tradition. In fact, he was sawn in half. Most modern Bible scholars saw his book in half too. That is to say, they speak of "First Isaiah" and "Second Isaiah" as two distinct persons. No one knows for sure. There are some good literary reasons for thinking that we do have two different authors here. But the three major arguments used to prove a double Isaiah are quite weak, it seems to me, without some qualification.

The first argument points to a difference in style and vocabulary between the two parts of the book. This is a strong clue, but it can prove there were two authors only if one author cannot write in two different styles. That is rare but possible. We do know of other literary examples of a two-style author.

A second argument points to an difference in the content between the emphasis on judgment in "First Isaiah" and the emphasis on forgiveness and hope in "Second Isaiah." This argument is theologically weak if it assumes that justice and mercy are opposed, not met together with a kiss (Psalm 85:10). As Aquinas points out, each of the divine attributes presupposes the other. For example, God's mercy in dealing with us, presupposes the justice that it surpasses.

It must be admitted, though, that the difference in content between judgment in "First Isaiah" and forgiveness in "Second Isaiah" is a strong argument *if* this difference (not contradiction) corresponds to two different historical situations. In this view, First Isaiah warns complacent, evildoing Israel of impending disaster and exile if they do not repent. On the other hand, Second Isaiah encourages people who have already suffered (probably suffered the exile) to hope for the future restoration of their land. Both these promises came true, then, from this view, but two hundred years apart.

A third argument for two Isaiahs is that the prophecies in the second part of the book couldn't have been written by First Isaiah, who lived long before the events described by Second Isaiah, because these events are described so specifically that the descriptions must be written by a contemporary. The key instance pointed to is the *naming* of King Cyrus of Persia as the one who would free the Jews from captivity in Babylon and allow them to return to Jerusalem.

Once again, this argument may be either weak or strong. It is weak if it assumes prophecy never really predicts the future, as it claims to, but only *pretends* to describe the future while really only describing the past or present. In other words, there's no such thing as predictive prophecy. Not only is this theologically heretical, it's also illogical, for it assumes the thing it's trying to prove. It begs the question.

But it is a strong argument for the two Isaiahs that the second part would not make sense to Israelites before the exile. No one would know who Cyrus was two hundred years before he was born. No other biblical prophecy *names* future individuals in this way. The two-Isaiahs, theory, then, does not necessarily deny that both Isaiahs miraculously prophesied the future. It just places Second Isaiah two hundred years closer to his prophecies' fulfillment.

In fact, *Isaiah* itself refutes the assumption that there's no predictive prophecy. For both Isaiahs, if there were two, lived long before Christ, yet the detailed prophecies of the life of Christ that we find in *Isaiah* are far more numerous and far more specific than the prophecies about anything else in the Bible. At least seventeen of them were fulfilled in remarkable detail.

Take the time to look up the following seventeen passages. These seventeen are only part of the more than three hundred different prophecies in the Old Testament that are fulfilled by Christ. Even though the New Testament writers (especially Matthew) deliberately used the style and language of Old Testament prophecies to describe events in the life of Christ—as a modern preacher might use King James English to describe current events—the statistical odds that one man could fulfill all of these prophecies so completely is not a lot better than the odds that a monkey could type out *Isaiah* by randomly throwing marbles at a typewriter keyboard.

1. Isaiah 7:14; Matthew 1:22-23.
2. Isaiah 9:1-2; Matthew 4:12-16.
3. Isaiah 9:6; Luke 2:11 (see Ephesians 2:14-18).
4. Isaiah 11:1; Luke 3:23, 32; Acts 13:22-23.
5. Isaiah 11:2; Luke 3:22.
6. Isaiah 28:16; 1 Peter 2:4-6.
7. Isaiah 40:3-5; Matthew 3:1-3.
8. Isaiah 42:1-4; Matthew 12:15-21.
9. Isaiah 42:6; Luke 2:29-32.
10. Isaiah 50:6; Matthew 26:26, 30, 67.
11. Isaiah 52:14; Philippians 2:7-11.
12. Isaiah 53:3; Luke 23:18; John 1:11; 7:5.
13. Isaiah 53:4; Romans 5:6, 8.
14. Isaiah 53:7; Matthew 27:12-14; John 1:29; 1 Peter 1:18-19.
15. Isaiah 53:9; Matthew 27:57-60.
16. Isaiah 53:12; Mark 15:28.
17. Isaiah 61:1-2; Luke 4:17-21.

Francis Bacon said, "Some books are to be tasted, others to be swallowed, and others to be chewed and digested." *Isaiah* is to be chewed, pondered, relished, and plunged into time after time after time. Like a smooth stone or an antique, it gets better, not worse, with wear.

NINETEEN

The Only Alternative to Disaster: Jeremiah and Lamentations

J EREMIAH IS CALLED "the weeping prophet." Expressions of woe and doom are called "jeremiads" because they are named after him.

But Jeremiah was just the opposite of our stereotype of the doomsayer: someone stern, severe, and sour, tight of jaw, bitter of bile, and hard of heart. Jeremiah was a sensitive, gentle, kind-hearted man; but God called him to deliver a harsh, hard message. God often calls us to necessities that we think our natural personalities are not fit for—perhaps so that it is clear that the deed is from him, not from us (see 1 Corinthians 1:18-29).

The "bottom line" of Jeremiah's message is so old and well-known that it is easily overlooked, like most profound platitudes. It is the truth that the only alternative to disaster is to "trust and obey," to surrender our will to God. Jeremiah had learned and lived this message—that's why God trusted him to deliver it—but Judah had not. And they were about to be destroyed by Babylon. They were like an overripe fruit about to fall off the tree when the winds came.

Jeremiah is a fine example of the rare but necessary combination of a soft heart and a hard will. He "set [his] face like flint" (Isaiah 50:7) to deliver God's message intact. But the task made his heart break into tears, for the message was judgment on the people both he and God loved dearly.

How do we know how God feels? Because the one who alone perfectly reveals the heart of God, the one in whom "all the fullness of God was pleased to dwell" (Colossians 1:19), showed us God's heart when he delivered the same message as Jeremiah's six centuries later and forty years before another destruction of Jerusalem and of the second temple, by the Romans in A.D. 70, which was to be followed by an even longer exile and dispersion of the Jews, until 1948. Here is Jesus' jeremiad:

> "O Jerusalem, Jerusalem, killing the prophets and stoning those who are sent to you! How often would I have gathered your children together as a hen gathers her brood under her wings, and you would not! Behold, your house is forsaken and desolate. For I tell you, you will not see me again, until you say, 'Blessed is he who comes in the name of the Lord!' " Matthew 23:37-39

No Old Testament poetry is more heartfelt and feeling-full than Jeremiah's, except some of the *Psalms*. A few of his expressions have become famous, such as: "Is there no balm in Gilead?" (8:22) and his personification of death as a grim reaper (9:21-22).

A MAN OF SUFFERING AND SEEMING FAILURE

He suffered in his own person as well as in sympathy for his people. He was homesick for his native countryside, but had to live and prophesy in the city. (He describes nature in great detail, especially animals.) He suffered throughout his long career for the dangerous habit of speaking the truth. He was rejected by his home town, unjustly tried and convicted, publicly humiliated, put into the stocks, threatened by false prophets, forced to flee for his life from the king. He spent seven years as a fugitive, and was thrown into a cold, wet well for his prison cell. Jeremiah was a political failure. It seemed that he was a spiritual failure as well, for his people did not heed his message.

But he was *not* a spiritual failure. For he remained obedient to God's command to "preach the word, be urgent in season and out of season" (2 Timothy 4:2). This "failure" verifies Mother Teresa's saying, "God did not put me on this earth to be successful, but to be faithful." This prisoner verifies C.S. Lewis' saying, "I was not born to be free, but to adore and to obey."

Jeremiah's unpopular message was not merely that the people were sinners—nothing new or startling there—but that they were *unrepentant* sinners, in fact smug and arrogant. ". . . no man repents of his wickedness, saying, 'What have I done?' Every one turns to his own course, like a horse plunging headlong into battle" (8:6). As for the false prophets, "from prophet to priest every one deals falsely. They have healed the wound of my people lightly, saying, 'Peace, peace' when there is no peace. Were they ashamed when they had committed abomination? No, they were not at all ashamed; they did not know how to blush" (8:10-12).

If God allowed reincarnation, I think Jeremiah would be the prophet he would bring back today. For the besetting sin of our society too is not so much any one particular sin—lust and greed and sloth and luxuriousness are hardly our invention—but the loss of the *consciousness* of sin. Our ancestors may have been more cruel than we, but at least they repented. They had no pop psychologists to whisper, "I'm okay, you're okay" and no pop religionists to whisper "Peace, peace" when there was no peace.

Or perhaps they did. And in Jeremiah's time they listened

to those popular false prophets. And the next step was as predictable as an equation in algebra. Divine justice is no more avoidable than mathematical justice.

Jeremiah reminds us of this equation, between sowing the wind and reaping the whirlwind (30:23; Hosea 8:7). God is patient, but his patience is coming to an end. He is not a wimp or a fool; he is not made in our image. Judah's disease was so far advanced that it could be dealt with only by radical surgery, the "severe mercy," the shock treatment, of the Babylonian exile. One cannot help wondering how Jeremiah would diagnose our civilization's advanced state.

Yet even the coming exile is mercy, for it (and it alone) would turn Judah's heart to seek God again, to listen and repent. As in the second chapter of Hosea, God has to bring his people into the wilderness (suffering) to remove their worldly distractions and pride so that in the silence of suffering and the shock of failure they can hear his voice again whispering the forgotten secret: that God is love, and this love must be jealous and demanding because our divine Lover is our only possible source of joy and life and liberation. God himself cannot change this fact: God is God and idols are idols. It's as ultimate as X is X and Y is Y.

There is always hope because God is always ready to be found. His love and mercy are as unchangeable as his justice and truth. Here is one of the most hopeful verses in Scripture: "You will seek me and find me; when you seek me with all your heart" (29:13; compare Matthew 7:8).

That, incidentally, is why God seems to hide from us. Why it is so hard to know or feel his presence and guidance; why "holy places are dark places," as C.S. Lewis put it. The source of light is the heart and we do not "turn on your heart-light." That's why a simple, unintellectual saint like Mother Teresa sees and says things of blinding clarity. That is why "intellectuals" and "experts" are often the blindest of the blind and the blandest of the bland. Light and fire come from the heart that bows to God, while darkness and ashes come from a god that bows to the demands of the human heart.

Jeremiah's hope is clearly messianic. God will fulfill the wonderful promises in chapter 31 only when the Messiah brings in the new covenant, written not on Moses' stone tablets or in a book, but in the blood of the sacred heart:

> Behold, the days are coming, says the LORD, when I will make a new covenant with the house of Israel and the house of Judah, not like the covenant which I made with their fathers when I took them by the hand to bring them out of the land of Egypt, my covenant which they broke, though I was their husband, says the LORD. But this is the covenant which I will make with the house of Israel after those days, says the LORD: I will put my law within them, and I will write it upon their hearts. 31:31-33

The Messiah *has* come, yet Jeremiah's messianic prophecy still applies to us, for he is also still to come and we are still to look forward, not backward. His first coming is to be completed by his second coming, and our baptism is to be completed by our sanctification. All growth in the Christian life begins at the place pointed out by Jeremiah's prophecy: in our admitting the Lord into more and more inner chambers of our heart (and therefore, inevitably, of our lives).

LAMENTATIONS:
JERUSALEM'S FUNERAL ORATION

Immediately following the *Book of Jeremiah* is a series of poems lamenting the destruction of Jerusalem and the temple. Imagine the Nazis had totally destroyed Rome, the Vatican, and all sacred shrines. Better, imagine the Eucharist disappeared from the face of the earth. This is how the Jews felt as Jeremiah composed Jerusalem's funeral oration in *Lamentations*.

Though the book does not name its author, the earliest Jewish and Christian traditions ascribe it to Jeremiah. The same tender heart is here. Instead of gloating, "I told you so" when his unheeded prophecies were fulfilled, he only weeps with his people.

The poems are acrostics: each verse begins with a different letter of the Hebrew alphabet in order. The author literally weeps from A to Z.

Hope arises not just *after* the tears but *out of* the tears. We see here the great Jewish and Christian mystery of the redemptive power of suffering. And we see that Judah's hope comes from the very same source as her judgment: from God. Her holocaust did not happen by chance, but by the justice of the same God who is the source of her mercy and hope. Because it was not the Babylonians but God at the source of her destruction, she has hope. For God, unlike Babylon, is also the source of her restoration. The same hope—the only one—is available to every sinner and sufferer and dying person today. The powers of darkness are ultimately controlled by the power of God. The solution to "the problem of evil" is: wait. God will bring good even out of evil, if only we turn to him:

> Remember my affliction and my bitterness,
>   the wormwood and the gall!
> My soul continually thinks of it
>   and is bowed down within me.
> But this I call to mind,
>   and therefore do I hope:
> The steadfast love of the LORD never ceases,

his mercies never come to an end;
they are new every morning;
   great is thy faithfulness.
"The LORD is my portion," says my soul. **3:19-24**

TWENTY

Two Supernatural Visionaries: Ezekiel and Daniel

T HE NAME "EZEKIEL" means "God strengthens." Ezekiel's style lives up to his name: it is both strong and supernatural. It reminds me of a Norse epic: high, remote, awesome, and wonderful. It is the Old Testament's closest equivalent to the dazzling otherworldly imagery of the Apocalypse.

Ezekiel was both a priest and a prophet. Yet he transcended the frequent conflict between these two groups of leaders in Israel. For he seems to write from a point of view higher than both. It is neither the priestly and liturgical nor the prophetic and moral, but his writings seem to echo from heaven itself, to which both liturgy and morality point.

He lived during the dark days of the Babylonian captivity and prophesied in Babylon to his fellow Jewish exiles. When he spoke his first prophecies of the destruction of Jerusalem and of Solomon's temple, Jerusalem had not yet been destroyed, though the Jews had already been taken captive to Babylon. When the Jews in Babylon heard the news of this destruction, they began to take Ezekiel seriously. He must have seemed like a madman to them before.

It was during this second stage of his prophetic career that Ezekiel spoke to the people expressly of hope, of a future return to the promised land, and of reconciliation with God. Like every true prophet of God, Ezekiel said two things, the bad news and the good news, sin and salvation. Whenever you hear either half of this message without the other, you know the messenger is not a true prophet.

EZEKIEL: GOD'S POWER AND GLORY IS DISPLAYED

The "sin" part of his message is both aweful and awful. Like all the prophets, he knows God as more than a comfortable chum. God is holy and unchangeably just. He cannot endure sin or compromise with it. Sin and God are like darkness and light; they cannot coexist. Therefore Ezekiel describes the visible cloud of God's glory, the *Shekinah,* leaving the temple, where it had been present since Solomon built it, and disappearing into the east, because the people's sins had driven it away. The name *Ichabod* comes from this event; it means "The glory has departed."

The *Shekinah* may have been present in Eden, permeating the bodies of Adam and Eve in visible divine light, until they sinned. That may be why they covered their now-naked, unlit bodies with clothes in shame. Ever since then, every sin is a little *Ichabod,* a darkening of our divine glory, our sending away the light of God.

Ezekiel's imagery is arresting, bizarre, terrifying, and supernatural. For instance, chapter 1 contains two visions of angels. Neither come from Hallmark; their hallmark is their heavenly origin. One is a vision of flying, four-faced, four-winged creatures in a storm of fire and lightning. The other vision is of wheels within wheels covered with eyes! Chapter 32 contains a vision of the world of the dead. And chapter 37 is a vision of a valley full of skeletons standing up and coming to life. Any Bible illustrator, cartoonist, or moviemaker who wants to fascinate small children should not ignore *Ezekiel*. The images burn themselves into our memory and touch something indefinable in our unconscious. They certainly banish boredom, one of the devil's most effective inventions.

Ezekiel's actions are almost as bizarre as his words, for both come from a supernatural source. God commands him to eat a scroll and to lie on the ground tied tightly with ropes, unable to talk (ch. 3); to lie on his left side in public for three hundred ninety days (ch. 4); and to burn his hair (ch. 5).

Ezekiel knew (or rather the God who inspired him knew) that "a picture is worth a thousand words"—that vivid symbols are unforgettable. Ezekiel's vision of the glory of God at the beginning (chs. 1-3) must have awed and overwhelmed him so deeply that this awe stuck to all that he said. It has an otherworldly but not imaginary feel, because it has an otherworldly but not imaginary origin. When I read *Ezekiel* I always think of Byzantine or Coptic liturgies, certainly not our modern Western warm fuzzies. Ezekiel would never use terminology like "building community" or "affirming values." He has seen something greater: the glory of God himself.

Though the power of *Ezekiel* is "primitive," the content of his message is quite "advanced" and sophisticated. He announces more clearly than any prophet before him the principle that each individual is responsible for and is justly punished for his or her own sins, not those of parents, ancestors, or the community (ch. 18). One wonders whether we are regressing to a pre-Ezekiel stage of moral wisdom in emphasizing the sinfulness of social structures more than the "little" sins of individuals today.

Ezekiel lived in a century (the sixth century B.C.) that has been called "the axial period in human history," because during this century God seems to have been sending a similar message to humanity throughout the world. Dramatists, philosophers, and poets like Aeschylus in Greece; mystics like Buddha in India; sages like Confucius and Lao Tzu in China; and prophets like Zoroaster in Persia were all turning their hearers inward to a new sense of self-consciousness. The external and social was becoming interiorized and individualized. Again, one wonders whether the next century will be the next "axial period in human history" when the turn reverses itself.

Like all the prophets, Ezekiel's "bottom line" is not doom but hope: hope for salvation, for new life, for a resurrection. The basis of this hope is not the human mind and wishful thinking, but the mind of God and divine revelation. The most memorable of the prophetic promises in *Ezekiel* is chapter 37, the famous vision of the dry bones coming to life.

This prophecy was fulfilled at Pentecost. It continues to be fulfilled as Pentecost occurs in the lives of individuals, in the life of the church, and potentially even in the whole world. Our world's slide down toward darkness can be reversed; the dead can live; the wind of the Spirit still blows from the four corners of the earth.

For this is the Spirit that brings to life dead Israel, dead orthodoxy, dead legalism, dead liturgy, dead Christians, and a dead world: the same Spirit who raised the dead body of Christ (Romans 8:11). It is Christ who fulfilled Ezekiel 37: see Luke 4:18 and John 7:37-39.

Other messianic prophecies in *Ezekiel* include the righteous king (21:26-27), the good shepherd (34:11-31), and the branch who grows into a tree (17:22-24; compare Isaiah 11:1; Jeremiah 23:5 and 33:15; and Zechariah 3:8 and 6:12). All prophecies are fingers pointing ultimately to Christ. All the words of all the prophets come down to a single Word, "The Word of God." In prophets like Ezekiel this Word was made into images, but in Christ the Word was made into flesh.

DANIEL: THE SWEEP OF HISTORY
FROM GOD'S PERSPECTIVE

The name "Daniel" means "God is my judge." He prophesied in Babylon to both Jews and Gentiles during the Babylonian captivity.

Some of the most famous and arresting stories in the Bible are found in this book, including the three young men in Nebuchadnezzar's fiery furnace (ch. 3), the "handwriting on the wall" written by a disembodied hand, prophesying the sudden doom at King Belshazzar's feast (ch. 5), and, of course, Daniel in the lions' den (ch. 6).

Most of the book is made up of visions of the future. These visions have a greater historical sweep than any other in the Old Testament, and predict four great world empires: the Babylonian, the Medo-Persian, the Greek, and the Roman.

There is a philosophy of history implied in Daniel's visions. It is that history is "his story" (God's). God is the Lord of history, planning and directing it as he plans and directs each life (even, we are told later, the fall of each sparrow and the numbering of each hair).

King Nebuchadnezzar had to go mad and live like an animal to learn this truth: "You shall be driven from among men, and your dwelling shall be with the beasts of the field; you shall be made to eat grass like an ox, and you shall be wet with the dew of heaven, and seven times shall pass over you, till you know that the Most High rules the kingdom of men, and gives it to whom he will" (4:25). "He changes times and seasons; he removes kings and sets up kings" (2:21).

The Messiah is prophesied in *Daniel* as a great stone who will crush all the kingdoms of the world, become a great mountain, and fill the whole earth (2:34-35). "And in the days of those kings [the Romans] the God of heaven will set up a kingdom [the church] which shall never be destroyed, nor shall its sovereignty be left to another people. It shall break in pieces all these kingdoms and bring them to an end, and it shall stand for ever" (2:44).

The four kingdoms recur in chapter 7, and so does the Messiah. Here, he is the "Son of Man" who receives from "the Ancient of Days" the kingdom "which shall not pass away" (7:13-14). Even the death of the "anointed one" is prophesied in Daniel 9:26, and perhaps even the exact time of this Messiah's coming, in the vision of "seventy weeks"— symbolically, 490 years—in Daniel 9:25 (though the state of the text is problematic here and gives evidence of later revisions).

TWENTY-ONE

More Mouths of God: The Rest of the Prophets

HOSEA: THE SUFFERING OF LOVE REJECTED

Of all the prophets, Hosea has perhaps the most tenderness and the most tragedy, both in his message and in his life. For Hosea exemplifies what is probably the greatest possible suffering, the suffering that hurt Christ more than any other: the suffering of love rejected.

God taught Israel the lesson of suffering love through Hosea, not only in words but also in deeds. He commanded Hosea to marry Gomer, an unfaithful woman, to show Israel their own unfaithfulness to God, and perhaps also something of what God felt in being spiritually betrayed by his chosen bride. "When the LORD first spoke through Hosea, the LORD said to Hosea, 'Go, take to yourself a wife of harlotry and have children of harlotry, for the land commits great harlotry by forsaking the LORD'" (1:2).

Love multiplies suffering by the factor of the quantity of that love. God's love is infinite. Therefore God can suffer infinitely. Christ's agony in the garden and on the cross was not just physical agony, it was the infinite agony of infinite love rejected, failed, unsuccessful. Those who object to the dogma of hell on the grounds that it would mean that man would suffer more than God, do not understand that God "descended into hell" on the cross and in the Garden of Gethsemane more deeply than any man could. The vision in the garden that so terrified Christ that he sweated bloody tears and asked his Father whether it was possible to avoid this "cup" was probably a vision of hell—a vision of all the human souls suffering eternal torment after having rejected Christ's love. *Hosea* is a dim foreshadowing of that.

After Hosea's personal suffering over his unfaithful wife taught him something of God's grief for his unfaithful people, and after this object lesson hopefully taught Israel the same truth, then Hosea forgave his wife and took her back—just as God forgives his people and takes them back time after time. When Jesus replied to Peter's question, "How often shall my brother sin against me and I forgive him? As many as seven times?" by answering, "I do not say unto you seven times, but seventy times seven," he was only preaching what he was practicing, throughout history. This too is foreshadowed in *Hosea:* "The LORD said to me, 'Go again, love a woman who is beloved of a paramour and is an adulteress; even as the LORD loves the people of Israel, though they turn to other gods' " (3:1). Love never gives up (1 Corinthians 13:8).

But forgiveness is compatible with punishment. God both forgives and punishes, for both are expressions of love (an essential lesson for parents). All God's punishments against Israel are out of love and for love, for the purpose of restoring and consummating the love between them, to bring her back to him and to joy. That is also what all punishments and all sufferings are. (Not that the two are identical: *Job* shows they are not.) In fact all the events in our lives are providentially designed for this end: to hedge us, prod us, inveigle us into God's marriage chamber. The whole story of the Bible, the whole story of human history according to the perspective of the Bible, is a love story.

It seems that it is not. Chapter 2 of *Hosea* is particularly profound in penetrating beneath the terrible appearance to the wonderful reality of life. It seems at first that Israel's (and our) sufferings are punishments from an angry God, a wronged husband. The language is harsh: "Upon her children also I will have no pity, because they are the children of harlotry" (2:4).

But the harsh treatment is really gentleness and compassion: "Therefore I will hedge up her way with thorns; and I will build a wall against her, so that she cannot find her paths. She shall pursue her lovers, but not overtake them" (2:6-7). The reason for God's inflicting suffering and failure on Israel, as on us, is to bring us to the point where we repent, turn, and return. The decision must be free, for love is by its nature free. But the sufferings and failures on the road of false, idolatrous loves that bring us to the point of free turning, are not freely chosen but inflicted against our will (but not against our eventual joy).

The point of the sufferings is explained in the next verse: "Then she shall say, 'I will go and return to my first husband, for it was better with me then than now.' And she did not know that it was I who gave her the grain, the wine, and the oil, and who lavished upon her silver and gold which they used for Baal. Therefore [to teach her this truth that she needs for her joy] I will take back my grain in its time, and my wine in its season" (2:7-9).

The arresting word that more than any other explains human suffering from the divine perspective of God wooing and winning his faithless human beloved, is the word "allure" in Hosea 2:14. Sufferings are part of God's allurements, God's courtship! "Therefore, behold, I will allure her and bring her into the wilderness, and speak tenderly to her." Only in the wilderness of suffering and silence can we hear the voice of God as it really is, quiet and tender and sweet and gentle. If God truly loves us, he *must* destroy the idols and the noise that we set up to block out the still, small voice of his love. For God *is* love (*agape*), and love, remember, never gives up (1 Corinthians 13:8).

Thus the most frequently heard reason for not believing in God—"If God loves us, why does he let us suffer?"—turns out to be one of God's supremely loving tricks. It is precisely because of God's love that we suffer, just as it is because of the dentist's charity that he drills the decay out of our teeth.

Hosea's name means "salvation." The word "Hosea" is closely related to the word "Joshua" and "Jesus." Hosea is a Christ-figure. The name is also closely related to the name of Israel's last king, Hoshea. The name is the message. Hosea saved and redeemed (bought back) his wife from the slave market (3:2) as God was to redeem his people from the slave market of sin, at the price of his own blood.

The story of Calvary has been repeated many times before and since. The whole Bible tells the same three-stage story: first, sin which is spiritual adultery (ch. 1); then the consequent suffering (ch. 2); then God's response of redemption (ch. 3). After the three-stage personal story is acted out on the stage of Hosea's life, the prophecy turns to its application to Israel and moves through the same three stages: chapters 4-7 show Israel's spiritual adultery, chapters 8-10 prophecy her coming captivity, and chapters 11-14 promise a future restoration to her land and to her relationship of fidelity and marriage to God. "Crime and punishment" make up only the first two-thirds of the story. And crime and punishment fit into, are part of, and are framed and explained by the ultimate point of the whole story—of Hosea, of Israel, of the Bible, of history, of life, of my life and yours: God's clever, tender, indefatigable courtship of our souls.

JOEL: JUDGMENT OR REPENTANCE—OUR CHOICE

Beginning with an account of a terrible plague of locusts which suddenly appeared in Judah like a storm cloud and destroyed every green plant in a single day, Joel announces God's judgment on sin. The locusts are only a warning, a mild version of the unthinkably terrible Last Judgment on the "day of the Lord" which will fall on all who are not repentant and right with God.

But disaster and threat are only half the truth. Famine, locusts, fire, invading armies, and the sun and moon blotted out are symbols of "the day of the Lord" for his enemies: "For the day of the LORD is great and very terrible; who can endure it?" (2:11). Yet the other half follows: "'Yet even now,' says the LORD, 'return to me with all your heart'" (2:12). "He is gracious and merciful" (2:13).

Joel's message is the same twofold point about God—justice and mercy, sin and salvation—found in all the prophets, in fact in all of Scripture. If readers find it tedious to have the same point repeated, they should remember: first, that it is poetry, not prose; song, not statistics. Poetry and song work by repetition or variations on the same theme. Second, we keep forgetting this simple lesson over and over, and need reminding over and over.

The most famous and important passage in *Joel* is his prophecy of Pentecost in chapter 2:28-32, which is quoted by St. Peter in Acts 2:16-21, when the prophecy is fulfilled. It was Christ who sent his Holy Spirit as he had promised (John 16:7-15; Acts 1:8), so this prophecy of Joel's was a messianic prophecy. It is also a worldwide, and not just a national, Jewish prophecy—a prophecy of the time when the God who had revealed himself to one "chosen people" would spread that knowledge through the church, throughout the world, and "all who call upon the name of the LORD shall be delivered" (2:32). *Joel* stresses the authority of God over all nations and all nature (that God sent the plague of locusts, for example), both to judge and to save.

AMOS: THE PROPHET WITH A MODERN BURDEN

Perhaps more than any other prophet, Amos seems to fit the picture of the "prophet of doom." Yet beneath his "doomsday" exterior, we can find many precious tidbits of positive wisdom. In these nine short chapters is contained an amazing amount of spiritual wealth and literary brilliance. One could easily write a whole book about Amos without being boring or repetitive.

His name means "burden," or "burden-bearer." For a prophet, as a holy man, loves the people to whom he must announce dooms, and this is the heaviest burden in the world, a burden only love can know.

Amos' burden is that beneath the appearances of prosperity, national optimism, contentment, and military power, Israel's soul was desperately sick, rotting from within. What the X-ray eyes of God see beneath the shine and shimmer is the last few swirls of garbage as Israel is about to go down the drain. The contemporary applications to America and to Western civilization, both in general and in detail, are terrifyingly appropriate. The sins Amos labels—lust, greed, religious infidelity and hypocrisy, arrogance, social injustice, materialism, and smugness—sound like the latest Gallup poll.

Amos was like John the Baptist: a rough, rude, unsophisticated country boy fearlessly "telling it like it is" to fashionable, sophisticated degenerates. He had not come from a line of clergy or professional prophets, but was a shepherd, farmer, and tree surgeon (7:14-15). But God took him by the hair of his soul and stood him up as a prophet. This divine call is the essential mark of the true prophet as distinct from the false or self-appointed prophet.

No prophet ever used stronger, bolder, sharper language than Amos. He had hard things to say, so he had to be a hard man to say them. Although God is compassionate, he is also hard, as unyielding as the moral law itself. Jesus manifests this hardness as well as tenderness—an extremely tricky and rare combination for most of us to live or even to like. Remember the hard things he said to the Pharisees or the money-changers in the temple. They don't nail a "nice guy" up to a cross and say he was a devil.

A religion that is a non-prophet organization is always less burdensome and more tempting. The real truth, and the real God, is always threatening and iconoclastic to the expectations and desires of fallen, sinful, self-indulgent human nature. Thus the society, in the person of the king and his private false prophet Amaziah, try to silence Amos (7:10-13), just as the media try to silence the church today. Not everyone who is controversial and hated is a prophet, but every prophet is controversial and hated. It is not true that to be misunderstood is to be great, but it is true that "to be great is to be misunderstood," as even Henry David Thoreau knew.

Amos used images from nature, just as Jesus did (he was a country boy too), such as the basket of rotten, overripe fruit (8:1-2) and fattened cows (4:1). Imagine calling a congregation *cows*—he obviously hasn't read *How to Win Friends and Influence People*. All his imagery is calculated to stir, to surprise, to shock.

I was once fired from a "homily service" (writing "model homilies" for priests) because I lacked the proper "tone": namely, always upbeat, quiet, and dignified. Amos never would have taken that job in the first place. He would have been a No-Doz pill in a tranquilizer factory.

Amos characterizes God as a roaring lion (1:2)—just as C.S. Lewis did with Aslan in his *Chronicles of Narnia*. We know God's tender side pretty well today, but we've forgotten his tough side. As Rabbi Abraham Heschel says, "God is not nice. God is not an uncle. God is an earthquake." Or, as Amos says, "Lo, he who forms the mountains and creates the wind, and declares to man what is his thought; who makes the morning darkness, and treads on the heights of the earth—the Lord, the God of hosts, is his name!" (4:13). The name is not Wimpy.

Prophets usually announce divine punishments. They also announce God's goodness. Only in modern times did anyone feel a tension, even a contradiction, between these two divine attributes. A God who tolerates evil, who does not punish, would not be good at all. True love and compassion are not tolerant of oppression and bullying (cf. 4:1, 6:5, 8:4-6). There are no "victimless crimes." And God loves the victim and hates the crime. Yes, God, the God who is love, hates (5:21). If you love your friend's body, you will hate the cancer that is killing it. And if God loves our souls, he must hate the sin that kills souls. Not to know this is not to know sin, not to know the soul, and above all not to know God.

God is more than just, but not less. His punishments are just and fit the crime and the degree of knowledge and responsibility. In the long catalog of crimes and punishments against the Gentile nations (chs. 1-2), they are held responsible for sins against the natural moral law known by all men by conscience. But Israel is held more responsible— responsible for sins against her special knowledge of God, her divine revelation (2:4-16).

One of the sins Amos denounces more vociferously than most moderns do is liturgical abuses (5:21-17). For liturgy is worship, obedience to the first and greatest commandment, according to both Mosaic and Christian reckoning (Exodus 20:3; Matthew 22:35-37). Liturgy is important because it is love—the love of God in action—and life—spiritual life, living communication between the divine and human lovers.

Amos also denounces sexual sins in the same breath as he denounces social and economic sins, as well as liturgical abuses (2:7-8). He is unlike most modern "prophets" of both Left and Right who confine themselves to a specialized and selective morality. Like the church centuries later, Amos "writes encyclicals" about all three areas of life. Sanctity is not a specialization. There's something in Amos, as in most of Scripture, to bother all of us. The saints always "comfort the afflicted and afflict the comfortable," as Dorothy Day put it.

Amos reserves his most severe and sarcastic jibes for the comfortable: "Woe to those who are at ease in Zion" (6:1). "Woe to those who lie upon beds of ivory ... who drink wine in bowls, and anoint themselves with the finest oils, but are not grieved over the ruin of Joseph!" (6:4-6). The most horrible state of all is a dead conscience. See Matthew 5:4 and Luke 6:25-6 on this.

Israel, God's chosen ones, will be punished more severely because they know God more: "You only have I known of all the families of the earth; therefore I will punish you for all your iniquities" (3:2). In this light, the claim to be God's "chosen people" is just the opposite of arrogant and triumphalistic. As one rabbi prayed, "Lord, couldn't you please choose somebody else from now on?" The same principle, of course, applies to the church, the New Israel.

Amos, like all the prophets, announces God's philosophy of history: the social parallel to Psalm 1's "two ways" leading inevitably to two different goals. Spiritual roads are just as objective as physical roads. You can't find blessing through sin or failure any more than you can find the Atlantic by going west from Chicago, or the Pacific by going east. This simple but constantly forgotten principle of history is borne out in the history of nations; not only Israel but also Babylon, Assyria, Greece, Rome, Germany, France, America.

And it works not just by divine intervention, miraculously, but by divinely instituted natural law, inevitably. Injustice is always terribly expensive, economically crippling. Sexual "freedom" destroys families and creates criminals. Oppression creates resentment and new oppressors. It's really amazing how stupid we are. God has to remind us again and again that nobody ever gets away with anything.

Amos pictures God as holding a plumb-line (7:7-8). God is "straight." Goodness itself isn't a little bad; light itself doesn't have even a tiny shadow in it. The God of the Bible has a character, a nature. This is the basis for morality: reflecting that character. "You shall be holy; for I the LORD your God am holy" (Leviticus 19:2). God's infinity does not mean he has no definite character, like a blob (that's pantheism, the Blob God). It means that each of his sharp and definite attributes is infinite: he is infinitely good, living, just, powerful, holy, wise, and so on.

Thus morality is never arbitrary, for it is based not only on God's law and word and will, but, in turn, on his nature, which is eternal and unchangeable. The popular misunderstanding of the message of the prophets is far too anthropomorphic and childish: God wants to be the boss; and when he sees people disobeying him, he gets upset and takes it out on them. This is how a spoiled child perceives a parent's loving discipline. Some of us never grow up.

The appropriate and inevitable punishment for refusing to heed God's Word is becoming incapable of hearing it: "I will send a famine on the land; not a famine of bread, nor a thirst for water, but of hearing the words of the LORD" (8:11). When a muscle is not exercised, it atrophies. The same is true of the spiritual ear.

Yet God will never abandon Israel, and Israel will never die (9:8). There are only two institutions in history that we know will still be around when history ends, even though they had definite beginnings in time: two exceptions to Buddha's supposedly universal principle that "whatever is an arising thing, that is also a ceasing thing." One is the church founded on the Rock of Peter. The other is Israel (see Romans 11).

OBADIAH: THE MESSAGE OF CRIME AND PUNISHMENT

The name "Obadiah," which means "servant of God," is quite common in the Old Testament. In fact, there are thirteen Obadiahs, and no one knows whether the writer of this book is the same as any one of the other twelve or not.

He prophesied to Edom, the nation which began with Esau, Jacob's brother. Esau's story can be found in Genesis 25-35. ("Esau" means "red," because Esau was red-haired.) The struggle between Jacob and Esau began before they were born, in their mother's womb (Genesis 25:22-26), and continued with their descendants, the nations of Israel and Edom. (God changed Jacob's name to "Israel." The Bible calls all his descendants "the children of Israel.")

Edom refused to help Israel when they were in the wilderness (Numbers 20:14-21) and also when they were conquering the promised land. Edom would not allow Israel to pass through its land. Many centuries later, one of Esau's descendants was King Herod. In Herod's attempt to murder Jesus (Matthew 2) the warfare between Edom and Israel continued.

Obadiah's prophecy of doom and total destruction for Edom (vv. 10, 18) came true in A.D. 70, when the Romans destroyed Jerusalem. The Edomites who fought them were not only defeated, but utterly lost to history. Obadiah's message is short and simple (his book is the shortest in the Old Testament: one chapter of 21 verses): "crime and punishment." Nations, like individuals, will reap what they sow. "The wages of sin is death."

JONAH: THE RELUCTANT PROPHET WHO DISCOVERED THE SCANDAL OF GOD'S MERCY

No one knows who wrote this book. (The book does not *say* that Jonah wrote it.) If the book is fact (history), Jonah is the obvious candidate. If it is fiction (parable), we have no clue to the author.

Like *Job* or the Cain and Abel story—*Jonah* is a borderline case between those books and passages in the Bible that clearly claim to be historical by their very style (for example, *Kings* or the four Gospels) and those passages that clearly have the form of moral parable rather than history, like the parables of Jesus).

A scholar who interprets *Jonah* as fiction is not necessarily a modernist or a demythologizer. It depends on his reason.

There are two possible reasons: one weak and one strong. If his reason is because the story centers on a miracle (Jonah alive in the belly of the "great fish"), then he is a modernist, for his hidden premise is that miracles can't happen in real history. This premise is 1.) heretical, 2.) irrational, and often even 3.) dishonest. It is heretical because the *essence* of Christianity is miraculous (creation, incarnation, resurrection). It is irrational because a God great enough to create the universe out of nothing is certainly great enough to preserve a man alive in a fish. And it is often dishonest because the real reason for interpreting a passage nonhistorically is seldom spelled out by the modernist theologian, but simply softly assumed, slipped in like a magician slipping a card up his sleeve.

A Fundamentalist has been defined as "one who believes in the credibility of Scripture and the edibility of Jonah." Probably the Fundamentalists are wrong in insisting on a literal interpretation of *Jonah*. But if they are, that is not because of the "great fish," but because of the literary form of the book. This is the second argument for interpreting *Jonah* as fable. Most Scripture scholars who are not Fundamentalists see it as a very strong argument.

"Form criticism" tells us to interpret each book within the framework of the literary form or genre that it exemplifies. If we are to properly use "form criticism," we will probably conclude that this book means to be parable, not history. In any case, we must not interpret this book, or any other, "in light of our own sincere beliefs." That is *eisegesis* or reading-into: reading *our* beliefs into the book. All good interpretation is *exegesis* or reading-out-of: reading the *author's* beliefs and intentions out of his book.

The strongest argument for interpreting *Jonah* as a fable or parable is that it has the literary form of the "tall story," full of satire, irony, humor, and "larger-than-life" exaggeration. (For instance, it describes Nineveh as a city so large that it takes three days to walk across it!) Also there are no other references to Jonah or Nineveh's conversion in any ancient literature, either Jewish or Gentile.

These are good reasons for thinking *Jonah* to be fable, similar to the reasons for thinking *Job* is fable. But many times bad literary reasons are given to suport this position

Some argue that *Jonah* is a parable because it teaches three moral lessons: 1.) that you can't run away from God, as Jonah tried to do; 2.) that even wicked people like the Ninevites can repent; and 3.) that God's mercy is for Gentiles (the Ninevites) as well as for Jews. But this argument surely does not prove *Jonah* to be mere parable, for God can teach moral lessons through real history as well as through invented parables. A moralist teaches moral lessons in the words he or she makes, but God teaches them also in the real events he providentially oversees. (History is "his story.")

But believing scholars who interpret *Jonah* as fable rather than history for literary reasons are *not* denying that miracles happen—or that God could not provide a nearly-miraculous "coincidence," like a great fish to swallow Jonah (survival in a whale maybe biologically possible). After all, *Exodus* says that the parting of the Red Sea (Reed Sea) was not caused simply by miracle but by a wind which God providentially arranged. The perfect timing is as striking an indication of God's presence and power as a supernatural miracle would be. The point of a miracle (the word means literally "sign") is precisely that anyway: to signify, to point beyond itself to God.

By the way, "three days and three nights" is a conventional Jewish phrase for *parts of* three days. It does not mean three times twenty-four hours, but could be as little as twenty-six hours (one hour of the first day, twenty-four of the second, one of the third). Jesus was dead from three in the afternoon on Friday to early Sunday morning, but this was reckoned "three days and three nights" even though it was only about thirty-nine hours, not seventy-two.

In the story, Jonah is called by God to be a prophet, a divine mouthpiece, to preach to Nineveh, the greatest and most wicked city in the world, the capital of the world empire of Assyria. Assyria had brutally and tyrannically held the civilized world in terror, captivity, and hatred for three hundred years. (And we think *we* have it hard preaching repentance to the modern pagan world? We have it easy compared to Jonah.)

God gives Jonah a one-word message: "Repent." God is a great economizer with words. Remember how incredibly brief Jesus was. Often, "more is less."

But Jonah hates the Ninevites and doesn't *want* to see them repenting and being forgiven and blessed by God. God's mercy is as scandalous to Jonah as God's justice is to many of us moderns.

So he runs away—or tries to. Instead of going east to Nineveh, he goes west to Tarshish (ancient Spain) by ship. He apparently doesn't know God well enough to know Psalm 139:9-10: "If I take the wings of the morning and dwell in the uttermost parts of the sea, even there thy hand shall lead me, and thy right hand shall hold me."

Of course no one can hide from God. Nothing in God's world can hide from God, any more than a character in *Hamlet* can hide from Shakespeare.

Ironically, every person and thing in the story obeys God except Jonah. The sailors fear God. The lots they cast tell the truth. The storm arises at God's will. The fish swallows Jonah when God calls it. The Ninevites repent when Jonah delivers God's Word. The plant grows up over Jonah when God commands it. The worm eats the plant when God brings it. Everything from large fish to worms obey God—everything except God's own prophet! We begin to see how this book is full of high and holy humor.

Jesus interpreted Jonah in the whale (or large fish, perhaps) as a symbol of his own death and resurrection: "For as Jonah was three days and three nights in the belly of the whale, so will the Son of man be three days and three nights in the heart of the earth" (Matthew 12:40).

Once Jonah obeys God and goes to Nineveh preaching repentance, the whole city obeys and repents! Which miracle is more startling and unbelievable—that a man finds physical life in the humble, dark place of a whale's belly, or that a whole nation finds spiritual life in the humble, dark place of repentance? Which miracle is more wonderful? The physical miracle, like all physical miracles, is not in itself important; its importance is that it points to the greater, spiritual miracle.

The lesson for prophets today is radically optimistic: despite ever-increasing signs of spiritual decadence in our world, repentance can come. Let us give our pagans a chance. Don't count them out. Tell them the unpopular truth that you feel sure they won't respect, believe, or obey, just as Jonah did. Then leave the results to God. Remember Mother Teresa's job description for a prophet: "God did not call me to be successful, but to be faithful."

Neither Jonah nor the Ninevites had the last word. God did, as usual. God writes the script. No matter how hard and hopeless our hearers' hearts seem, no matter how hard and hopeless our own hearts may be (like Jonah's), it is God who gives the grace. "With men it is impossible. But with God all things are possible."

When Nineveh repents, Jonah sulks. So God teaches him something about his own divine nature, full of love and compassion—by a plant, a worm, and a wind. (Children need simple, concrete lessons.)

Please don't miss the almost slapstick humor in this book. The whole tone is misinterpreted if you miss this, as so many miss the irony and satire in many of the sayings of Jesus. Jonah needs a *fish* to bring him to where God commands! Just picture the comic scene of this reluctant prophet vomited up from a fish, his skin white and blotched from its belly, dripping with vomit, stalking through the wicked city reluctantly mumbling his one-word message which he hopes will fail, and which succeeds! The reluctant prophet is the most instantaneously successful preacher in the Bible. His one word converts the greatest and most wicked city in the world.

The irony continues in the last chapter when God shows Jonah, through sending the worm to eat the plant that sheltered him from the sun, that Jonah has more compassion on a plant than on a city—a city which God describes as full of people "who do not know their right hand from their left" (4:11). Then the last line: ". . . as well as many animals." Even animals seem to share in human sin and repentance somehow. God cares about them too. In fact, God loves animals more than Jonah loves people!

The serious lesson in the humor (humor is often profoundly serious) is that God can and does use anything and everything: a worm, a wind, a whale, even a Jonah. He's not proud. How dare we be?

MICAH: HIS MESSAGE IS "WHO IS LIKE GOD?"

His name is an abbreviation for "Who is like God?" His message is his name: "Who is a God like thee?" (7:18).

Micah has three messages from God. First, he tells of the sins of Judah and Israel. Second, he predicts their punishment. And third, he announces hope for the future, a restoration of the people to their homeland and a reconciliation with God. These are essentially the three messages of all the prophets.

The most famous verse in *Micah* summarizes God's demands, the reasonable demands which were being ignored: "He has showed you, O man, what is good; and what does the LORD require of you but to do justice, and to love kindness, and to walk humbly with your God?" (6:8).

In chapters 6 and 7, Micah imagines God and his people debating in court and God calling them to account, setting forth his case. The whole universe, nature itself, is the jury. The verdict is guilty—guilty of violating the two great commandments, love of God with all one's heart and love of neighbor as one's self. The first has been replaced with false, empty, external, and hypocritical worship. The second has been replaced with injustice: oppression, bribery of judges, priests and prophets, exploitation, greed, cheating, pride, and violence.

The third message, the hope for true peace, justice, and happiness, depends on the coming of the Messiah. Micah 5:2 is one of the clearest and most specific of the Old Testament prophecies. It pinpoints the birthplace of the Messiah as Bethlehem. This was written about seven hundred years before Jesus was born. The scribes quoted it in Matthew 2:5-6 to try to prove that Jesus wasn't the Messiah, because they thought he had been born in Nazareth, not Bethlehem. They didn't know Jesus, but they knew their Old Testament well.

NAHUM: THE DESTRUCTION OF NINEVEH

Nahum prophesied the doom of Nineveh a century after Jonah preached to it. Its repentance did not last. Total

168 / You Can Understand the Old Testament

destruction is prophesied, and fulfilled: not a trace of the city remained after the next great world empire, Babylon, destroyed it.

Nineveh seemed like the *Titanic*: unsinkable. It was the mightiest city on earth, with walls one hundred feet high and wide enough for three chariots side by side. Towers on the walls rose up two hundred feet, and there was a moat around the wall sixty feet deep and one hundred fifty feet across. It seemed to the world absolutely invincible. But as Nahum predicted, "a great rushing flood" destroyed the city, flattening its wall. And the Babylonians entered to burn and plunder it. The site of the city was so thoroughly destroyed that it was not found until A.D. 1842, 2454 years later.

The destruction of Nineveh was not only Babylon's doing, but God's doing. God used the Babylonians, but it was his hand that defeated Nineveh, because Nineveh had made itself God's enemy by making itself the enemy of God's people. It was God's kindness to his people that was the reason for his destruction of their enemies: "The LORD is good, a stronghold in the day of trouble" (1:7).

HABAKKUK: GOD WRITES STRAIGHT
WITH CROOKED LINES

This man with the unusual name writes an unusual book about a common topic, the great question of evil. Just as with *Hosea*, we find here a startling turnaround of our ordinary ways of looking at evil, and we see God, the totally good and totally loving one, using evil and suffering to abolish evil and suffering. *Hosea* and *Habakkuk* form a dramatic two-part answer to the "problem of evil."

In *Hosea* the emphasis is on love, on how the God of pure love uses punishment and suffering to further his love-plan. In *Habbakuk* the focus is on justice, on how the God of pure justice allows the injustice of "the bad guys" defeating "the good guys," in order best to effect ultimate justice in history. *Hosea* looks at evil and good, betrayal and fidelity, suffering and joy, in the lives of individuals as well as nations, in terms of ultimate love. *Habakkuk* looks at evil and good, injustice and justice, in the lives of nations, on the stage of world history.

The book takes the form of a dialog with God. *Habakkuk* begins with a common and natural complaint against God. If we are honest, we must admit that we frequently share this complaint against God for not using his power to defeat the evils in the world more quickly and decisively. The book begins with the poignant cry:

> O LORD, how long shall I cry for help, and thou wilt not hear? Or cry to thee "Violence!" and thou wilt not save? Why dost thou make me see wrongs and look upon trouble? Destruction and violence are before me; strife and contention arise. So the law is slacked and justice never goes forth. For the wicked surround the righteous, so justice goes forth perverted. 1:2-4

God's reply is startling: "Look among the nations, and see; wonder and be astounded. For I am doing a work in your days that you would not believe if told. For lo, I am rousing the Chaldeans, that bitter and hasty nation, ..." (1:5-6). God is using evil to defeat evil, using the cruel Babylonians (Chaldeans) to punish Israel for her crimes, washing Israel clean from her dirt by the very dirty work of the Babylonians.

This scandalizes Habbakuk even more: "Thou who art of purer eyes than to behold evil and canst not look on wrong, why dost thou look on faithless men, and art silent when the wicked swallows up the man more righteous than he?"

(1:13). Granted, Israel is wicked, but Babylon is more wicked still. Why let the bad guys win?

Habakkuk gets an answer because he combines two essential means to hear and discern God's will and word: a strong will and a silent mind. He says, "I will take my stand to watch, and station myself on the tower, and look forth to see what he will say to me" (2:1). He knows the essential preliminary to wisdom: worship. And he knows the necessary preliminary to worship: silence. "The LORD is in his holy temple; let all the earth keep silence before him" (2:20). The Anglican Book of Common Prayer begins its liturgy with this verse and this attitude.

God's answer is, in a word, "Wait."

And the LORD answered me:
"Write the vision,
make it plain upon tablets,
so that he may run who reads it.
For still the vision awaits its time;
it hastens to the end—it will not lie.
If it seem slow, wait for it;
it will surely come, it will not delay." 2:2-3

As St. Augustine says, in answering the "problem of evil," "Since God is the highest good, he would not allow any evil to exist in his works unless his omnipotence and goodness were such as to bring good even out of evil" (*Enchiridion* 11). We're in a fairy tale, and we're only at the place where Snow White has eaten the poisoned apple, not yet at the point where she wakes and marries the Prince. God is writing a perfect script, but "God writes straight with crooked lines."

What will come in the end out of injustice is justice: "Behold, he whose soul is not upright in him shall fail, but the righteous shall live by his faith" (2:4). What is promised here is nothing less than the gospel. The gospel of eternal life through faith is more than justice, but not less.

The other side of salvation by faith is damnation by faithlessness. Chaldea will reap what she sows, and this is the second part of the vision God shows Habakkuk. No one gets away with anything. Babylon will reap the fruit she sowed: greed (2:5-11), cruelty and violence (2:12-17), and idolatry (2:18-20)—three very modern sins. When Habakkuk hears that God will punish his enemies, he pleads for mercy, not justice: "thy work, O LORD, do I fear. . . . in wrath remember mercy" (3:2).

Habakkuk began by questioning God and asking for justice; he ends by adoring and praising God's wisdom and power and justice (3:3-15), and pleading for mercy. At the end we find the prophet who had loudly complained about God's silence and delay "quietly [*waiting*] for the day of trouble" (3:16) and "[rejoicing] in the LORD . . . joy in the God of my salvation" (3:18). For God has taken Habakkuk to a high place to see a high vision of divine purposes in human history. He has taken him to a mountaintop: "God, the Lord, is my strength; he makes my feet like hinds' feet, he makes me tread upon my high places" (3:19). It is a foreshadowing of the vision of life's meaning that the saints have now and the blessed will have in heaven. It is meant to inspire us amid the muddle and the muck: "so that he may run who reads it" (2:2).

ZEPHANIAH: THE DAY OF WRATH

"Zephaniah" means "one whom God has hidden." He was the great-great grandson of King Hezekiah—a prince as well as a prophet—and was hidden from the evil king Manasseh. After Manasseh, Judah was blessed with a good king, Josiah, whose reforms were probably urged on him by the prophet Zephaniah.

Zephaniah prophesied just before the Babylonian captivity. Despite Josiah's reforms, the people's hearts were still corrupt, and needed purgation and punishment. God is kind but severe. Zephaniah, like all the writers of Scripture, sees both aspects of God. Though most of his prophecy is dark and full of doom, grim and grey, yet a light dawns when he looks beyond the time of punishment to a time of joy when God will "deal with all your oppressors" (3:19), a time to "rejoice and exult with all your heart" (3:14).

A prophecy can have more than one meaning. The "day of the Lord" prophesied by many Old Testament writers can refer to: 1.) an event in Old Testament times, such as the Babylonian captivity or the return from it; 2.) the great event of New Testament times, the coming of the Messiah; or 3.) the second coming of the Messiah at the end of the world. Sometimes it can mean all three. The passage in Zephaniah 3:9-10 is a good example.

Zephaniah's central message is the same as that of all the prophets: "Seek the LORD [or "repent" in other translations], all you humble of the land, who do his commands; seek righteousness, seek humility; perhaps you may be hidden [literally, 'be hidden'—Zephaniah's own name] on the day of the LORD" (2:3).

The writer of the famous medieval hymn "Dies Irae" ("Day of Wrath") based his description of the day of judgment on Zephaniah's prophecy.

HAGGAI: CALL TO REBUILD THE TEMPLE

Haggai speaks plainly and directly, with no rhetoric or oratory, to the Jews who had returned from exile in Babylon to Jerusalem. They had not rebuilt the great temple for sixteen years. They had put their own business ahead of God's. Haggai encourages them to build God's temple by telling them God's promise to be with them, and reminding them of God's sovereign power over nations and history.

The message was needed because the Jews who returned to Jerusalem from Babylon were discouraged. Their land was desolate. Crops failed. Work was hard. And the Samaritans, their neighbors on the north, hindered their work. So they stopped building. (The background story to Haggai is found in Ezra 4-6.) Haggai and Zechariah both urged them to finish, and succeeded. Haggai is one of the few prophets who lived to see his dream fulfilled.

However, according to the Jewish Talmud, the new temple was inferior to the old because it did not contain the ark of the covenant or the *shekinah* (the cloud of glory that showed God's presence). But the temple had to be built because the Messiah was due to come to it. Malachi 3:1 prophesied that. That is why Haggai said "the latter splendor of this house shall be greater than the former" (2:9). It was filled with the glory of God himself in the flesh when Christ came to Jerusalem and taught in the temple.

Haggai 2:6-8 is famous because Handel included it in his "Messiah." It probably refers to both the first and the second coming of Christ:

I will shake the heavens and the earth and the sea and the dry land; and I will shake all nations, so that the treasures of all nations shall come in, and I will fill this house with splendor, says the LORD of hosts. The silver is mine, and the gold is mine, says the LORD of hosts.

ZECHARIAH: SYMBOLS, VISIONS, AND MESSIANIC PROPHECIES

The time and setting for *Zechariah* is the same as that for *Haggai*. Zechariah prophesied to the exiles returning to Jerusalem from Babylon. His name is one of the most popular in the Old Testament (there are twenty-nine different Zechariahs) and means "God remembers." His theme is that God remembers his covenant promises to bless Israel. Zechariah was murdered in the temple (Matthew 23:35) just as another Zechariah had been (2 Chronicles 24:20-21). (Prophets would have found it hard to get life insurance.)

Zechariah's language is in sharp contrast to Haggai's plain and simple style. It is full of symbols and visions: riders on red, white, and dappled horses among myrtle trees (1:7-17); four ox horns and workmen with hammers (1:18-21); a man with a measuring line (2:1-13); the high priest standing before an angel (3:1-10); a golden lampstand (4:1-14); the flying scroll (5:1-4); a woman in a basket (5:5-11); and the four chariots (6:1-8). Zechariah also speaks more about angels than any other Old Testament writer.

Chapters 9 to 14 look far into the future, foretelling that Israel's neighbors would be conquered (by Alexander the Great), but that Israel would be spared for the coming of the Messiah (9:9-10), her King and Shepherd whom she would reject (11:4-17). Chapters 12 to 14 refer to Christ's second coming and the end of the world. *Zechariah* is full of messianic prophecies (3:1-2; 3:8-9; 6:12-13; 9:9-10; 10:4; 11:4-13; 13:1; 13:7), some of them extremely specific, such as the Messiah's being sold for 30 pieces of silver (11:13) and his triumphal entry into Jerusalem (on Palm Sunday) on a donkey (9:9).

MALACHI: GOD HAS BEEN NEGLECTED, AND EVILDOERS WILL NOT GO UNPUNISHED

His name means "my messenger" or "messenger of God." His book prophesies the coming of "my messenger to prepare the way for me, and the Lord whom you seek will suddenly come to his temple" (3:1). This "messenger" was John the Baptist (see Isaiah 40:3), who prepared the way for Christ. John would not appear for over four hundred years. Malachi is apparently the last Old Testament prophet—

unless *Daniel* was written much later than the rabbinic tradition has believed. He is followed by four hundred years of silence from God. The silence was broken by John the Baptist's voice quoting Isaiah 40:3 (Matthew 3:3). Jesus called John the greatest of the prophets (Matthew 11:11). Malachi may have been the closest to him in time. He is at least the closest to him in the pages of the Bible.

The problem Malachi addressed in his own time was smugness and a false sense of security. Even many of the priests were corrupt, and many people questioned whether it paid to obey God, since the wicked seemed to prosper. Their attitude was not simple and clear rebellion against God, but coldness of heart, materialistic dullness and dryness and dimness of spirit, and legalism. This was just the type of attitude that, according to Matthew's Gospel, the Pharisees and Sadducees showed in Jesus' day and that Jesus condemned as harshly as the prophets did.

Malachi addresses this problem in a question-and-answer form, as a dialog with God. His answer to the great problem of evil (if God is just, why do the wicked prosper and the righteous suffer?) is first of all that the people have neglected God, God has not neglected them. Second, their evil will not go unpunished, as the history of Edom shows. As with *Habakkuk,* the answer to the problem of evil is: "wait." The "day of the Lord" will come, and then it will be clear that it is not "vain to serve God" (3:14).

Malachi (and the whole Old Testament) ends by mentioning Moses (4:4) and Elijah (4:5), who appeared with Christ on the Mountain of Transfiguration (Matthew 17:3). The promise to send an Elijah (4:5) was fulfilled by John the Baptist (Matthew 17:10-13), who prepares for "the great and terrible day of the Lord," the coming of Christ. The whole Old Testament has been like an arrow, and here is its tip, pointing to the center of the target, the center of all things (Colossians 1:17), Christ.

TWENTY-TWO

History, Wisdom, and Even Apocalyptic Visions: The Deuterocanonical Books and the Apocrypha

THE FOLLOWING BOOKS AND parts of books are listed separately because they are "Deuterocanonical." That means they are the "second canon (list of sacred writings)." They were added later to the canon of the Old Testament, both by the Jews (in Greek Alexandria) and the early Christian church.

The Deuterocanonical Books were only written in Greek and not in Hebrew. This is one reason why Protestants and the Jews of Palestine do not include them in their Bible. But the same Catholic church that defined the first canon also declared the second to be inspired at the Council of Trent. The Orthodox churches of the East also accept them as canonical with the exception of *Baruch*.

TOBIT: GOD'S PROVIDENTIAL CARE

Delightful, charming, enchanting in its simplicity—these are some of the characteristics critics find in the story of *Tobit*.

Like most storytellers of the past, its writer set his tale in days gone by, in Nineveh, the capital city of the Assyrian empire. There, in exile from his native Israel, lived Tobit, a good Jew (his name means "the good"), who goes blind because of a very peculiar accident. The story centers on the journey of his son Tobias into far-away Media to reclaim a fortune Tobit had left there, with the help of a disguised angel Raphael and even a faithful little dog who makes the whole journey with them. In Media there lives the beautiful but unfortunate Sara, whose seven husbands all died on their wedding night, slaughtered by the demon Asmodeus. But the angel Raphael knows how to deal with demons and tells Tobias how to cast out Asmodeus with a fish's liver!

In addition to these supernatural elements, there are many realistic details, like Tobit's wife's irritation at her husband's scrupulous honesty, her anxiety for his blindness, which forces her to take in sewing to support the family, her constant watching the road for her son's return, and old Tobit counting the days.

Is the story meant as fiction or fact? We cannot decide it is fiction simply by pointing to the supernatural elements, for the whole of the Jewish and Christian religions are based on a supernatural and miracle-working God. But the literary style of the story is very different from the historical books, and it is probably meant to be taken as a "tall tale." Whether history or parable, biography or fiction, its lessons are true, for they are those of the rest of God's Word: faith and trust in God's providential "tender loving care" always pays off in the end.

JUDITH: A COURAGEOUS WOMAN
DELIVERS HER PEOPLE

The name "Judith" comes from the Hebrew "Jehudith" and means "Jewess." She is the heroine of a story whose historical background is hard to place accurately, since names, places, and dates seem out of historical order and treated very freely and loosely. But its point is not history but character.

Judith is a widow. Her husband died of sunstroke three years before the story begins, and she is still in mourning. The Jewish nation is in danger of being destroyed by an enemy army. Her city Bethulia is under siege, and the evil king Nebuchadnezzar's general-in-chief Holofernes has cut off its water supply. The despairing citizens beg their rulers to surrender, but Judith has a better plan. Her courage and strong faith in God contrast with their cowardice.

She takes off her mourning clothes and makes herself so beautiful that she is sure to "entice the eyes of all men who might see her" (10:4). Then she brings gifts to the camp of Holofernes, wins his confidence, and eventually wins his head, which she cuts off and brings home in a food bag. The drunken braggart and bully is defeated by the charm and wit of a woman, and the mighty army of Holofernes is defeated in a rout. Thus King Nebuchadnezzar's plans are frustrated. His ambition was to conquer the whole world and destroy all religions that did not worship him. Some commentators see Judith in her beheading of the evil Holofernes as a foreshadowing of Mary as the new Eve crushing the head of the serpent, or Satan, the one who does desire to conquer the world and destroy all true religion. Judith is the Jewish Joan of Arc. Too bad she was not around to deal with Hitler.

ESTHER (GREEK VERSION):
THE RELIGIOUS INTERPRETATION

This is the same story as the Hebrew *Book of Esther* (see page 90), but with some additions. The religious lesson here is not left implicit in the events as it was in the Hebrew version, but made explicit in the Greek author's comments.

In *Esther,* as in the *Genesis* story of Joseph, God makes no outward or miraculous manifestations of his power. Rather he directs events by natural causes, yet brings good out of evil in the end, justice out of injustice, and shows that "in everything God works for good with those who love him" (Romans 8:28). The lesson that success comes from trusting in God's providence and plan is like the bones of the original *Esther* story (see Esther 14:14). The Greek additions are like an X-ray that makes the bones prominent, makes the religious structure and meaning of the events clear.

THE WISDOM OF SOLOMON: THE GOD BEHIND THE LAW

This book was written not by King Solomon, but by an unnamed Jewish writer a century or two before Christ who seems to have lived in the Greek city of Alexandria, in Egypt, the world's center of Greek learning at the time. The title was not meant to deceive anyone, but to express the author's admiration for Solomon and to claim to be his disciple and imitator of his wisdom.

The book is a synthesis of ideas from Jewish religion and Greek philosophy and literature. Its main lesson is the same as that of the rest of the Old Testament: justice and fidelity, God rewarding those who are faithful to his law. This fidelity is the heart of wisdom. The book clearly affirms God to be all-just, all-knowing, all-good, and the origin only of good: "God did not make death, and he does not delight in the death of the living" (1:13)—a theme already taught in Genesis 3, where death is the result of sin, not of God.

In *Wisdom,* the perfections of God reach a new high point of theological development, and the author reflects on the lessons which the history of God's people have taught about the nature of God and the nature of wisdom. The understanding of God's character and intentions grows throughout Jewish history, just as a plant, an animal, a human body, or a human mind grows. For instance, the later prophets of Israel emphasized the need for personal virtue and not just external observance of the law. They place more responsibility on the individual since increased knowledge brings increased responsibility.

"Wisdom" here means not merely the practical ability to succeed well in life, or even the art of behaving ethically, but spiritual vision, understanding of God and his role in our lives and history. This wisdom had been deepening among God's people for two thousand years, all leading up to one point: the time when the complete and perfect understanding of God would once for all become available to the whole world in Christ, God's Wisdom incarnate. The best wisdom of all the ages was a series of pointing fingers or signs to him. "Wise men still seek him."

ECCLESIASTICUS: THE TEACHINGS OF A GREAT SAGE

This fifty-one-chapter book is the longest among the Deuterocanonical books. Its author, Jesus (or Joshua) ben (son of) Sirach, was a teacher, scholar, and poet in Jerusalem about one hundred eighty years before Joshua ben Joseph, Jesus the Messiah. This book is probably a series of lectures he gave in the school that he ran in that city.

His writing seems to indicate that he had traveled and studied widely about other countries and observed life carefully in order to build up his own philosophy of life. Most of the book resembles *Proverbs* in being realistic and practical. Its most beautiful chapters are the most poetic ones: 1, 24, 38, and 43.

The basic theme is a defense of Jewish wisdom and the claim that God has given it: "all wisdom comes from the Lord" (1:1). This claim, repeatedly made by Jewish writers in the Old Testament does not mean "listen to me because I'm as wise as God," but rather "whatever wisdom I have, give God the credit for it, not me." It is like the claim to be God's chosen people: a claim that seems arrogant, but is really the most humble interpretation of the fact that the Jews *are* really different. It ascribes their greatness to God, not themselves, and turns our attention from them to him: "To fear (respect) the Lord is the first step to wisdom" (1:14).

In chapter 24 wisdom is personified, much as in *Proverbs* (see chapter on *Proverbs*). These words of Jesus son of Sirach could well be seen as applying to another Jesus, whom "God made our wisdom" (1 Corinthians 1:30).

BARUCH: SPEECHES GIVEN TO THE EXILES IN BABYLON

Baruch was Jeremiah's scribe or secretary. This book contains four short speeches by Baruch given to the Jewish exiles in Babylon. Their effect on the people was moving: "Everyone cried, fasted, and prayed to the Lord. Then everyone gave as much money as he could and the collection was sent to Jerusalem" (1:5-7). When you read it, imagine *you* are a poor, defeated, powerless Jewish exile in Babylon and that you believe this as the long-awaited message from God to give new hope to you and your defeated nation. Note especially the inspiring poetry at the end (4:36-5:9).

THE LETTER OF JEREMIAH: THE FAILURE OF IDOLATRY

The first verse explains the source of this book: Jeremiah the prophet sends a letter to the people of Jerusalem who are about to be captured and taken into exile in Babylon. The prophet foretells this and interprets it as God's necessary punishment on the people's foolish idolatry. It was foolish both for knowledge (confusing the living God with a dead idol—but this applies to dollar bills just as much as to stone statues) and for practice (for since the idols have no power to save, those who trust in them will not be saved). The result of idolatry in practice is always failure, like leaning on a broken crutch.

THE PRAYER OF AZARIAH AND
THE SONG OF THE THREE YOUNG MEN

This addition to the *Book of Daniel* is found in the later, Greek version of *Daniel*. The "Song" is a cosmic canticle of praise which the three young men sing from the middle of the fiery furnace into which the evil king Nebuchadnezzar had thrown them when they refused to worship him (Daniel 3). In the song, all of creation praises God, from snow to snails. "Inanimate" matter and "dumb" animals are living works of art which loudly praise their divine artist, just as a good song praises its composer or a great play praises its playwright.

This canticle was for a long time well known and loved in the church's public liturgy, and is still loved and used by many in private prayer. It brings prayer into the realm of the concrete world when we call on specific things like whales and stars and heat to praise God. It is an application of Psalm 150, which commands *everything* to praise God. All goodness is God's goodness, all truth is God's truth, and all beauty is God's beauty.

SUSANNA: AN INNOCENT WOMAN IS VINDICATED

This is a short story of the same kind as *Tobit* and *Judith*: simple, full of surprises, and enchanting. A beautiful woman, Susanna, is falsely accused by two jealous, evil judges and saved by the young judge Daniel, who shows Solomon-like wisdom. It is one of the earliest forerunners of the modern detective story. Though only one chapter long, it contains many memorable details, such as the two trees which are silent witnesses for Susanna. Once you start the story, you cannot put it down until the end.

Like *Tobit*, this story seems to have the literary form of fable rather than history. I think one should not be too dogmatic either way. But the literary style is like that of *Tobit* and *Bel and the Dragon*, rather than straightforward historical narrative like *Maccabees*.

BEL AND THE DRAGON: THREE DETECTIVE STORIES

These are three stories which the later Greek version of the Hebrew Scriptures added to the *Book of Daniel*. All three are exciting detective stories, or "thrillers." The first two center on Daniel and his wisdom in overcoming an idol set up by the Babylonians, who had destroyed Jerusalem and taken the Jews into captivity in Babylon. In the first story, Daniel exposes a clever technological trick by a trick of his own and proves that the idol Bel did not magically eat the food offered to it, as it appeared. In the second story, Daniel destroys a great live dragon (perhaps a giant crocodile) which the Babylonians worshiped, without using any weapons. The point of both stories is not only Daniel's cleverness, but also the foolishness of worshiping idols of any kind, that is, anything in the world except the one true God.

The third story is an addition to the story of Daniel in the lion's den. It tells of the prophet Habakkuk, an interrupted stew, and an angelic air transportation by the hair from Israel to Babylon to feed Daniel Habakkuk's stew as the lions watched, hungrily, waiting until Daniel's enemies were thrown into their den. Then they had their just desserts.

FIRST MACCABEES: RESISTANCE AGAINST TYRANNY

This is a historical book which tells of the Jewish struggle for religious and political freedom from the Greek empire of the Seleucid kings who had inherited the world from Alexander the Great. The Maccabees are a Jewish family chosen by God to stand up against the tyrant Antiochus Epiphanes ("that wicked root"), who persecuted the Jews and blasphemously desecrated the temple. This tyrant stole its holy treasures and set up altars to heathen gods, tore and burned the sacred books of the law, and mistreated any Jewish women who had their baby boys circumcised in obedience to Jewish law.

The first two chapters of the book set up the two sides of the war as irreconcilable enemies. On the one hand, the Greek rulers insisted not only on political conquest of Israel and the removal of political freedom, but also religious persecution and instituting practices the Jews considered blasphemous, especially in the temple. Many Jews compromised with the Greek conquerors and even helped them. On the other hand, those Jews who remained faithful to God, his law, and his temple worship resisted Antiochus Epiphanes, both by force and by martyrdom.

The rest of the book is the story of three resistance movements, one for each of the sons of Mattathias: Judas Maccabeus, "The Hammerer," and his brothers Jonathan and Simon, who each led the resistance in turn and were killed in turn. It is a story of war, intrigue, and murder—full of detailed descriptions of ancient warfare, including mounted engines to throw fire and rocks, and elephants with towers of wood. Yet even in this bloody time God's hand is seen, testing his people, punishing them with national suffering only in order to bring them back to himself, and aiding those who were loyal to him. The Maccabees, like the Jews of older times, succeed only by God's help and fail only when they turn away from God.

God's providence over history was keeping the nation of Israel alive, against all ordinary odds, because they were his chosen people, mail carriers to the whole world of his revelation, of the true knowledge of who God really is. They were the people from whom his promised Messiah was to come. These dark years, full of wars and violence, without a prophet from God for four hundred thirty years between Malachi and John the Baptist, were the dark before the dawn.

SECOND MACCABEES:
PRAISE FOR MARTYRS OF THE FAITH

This book covers part of the same period covered by *First Maccabees*. It is the story of the Jewish fight for Jerusalem and the temple, for political and religious independence. There is some overlapping, and many of the same events are told from another point of view. The style here is more like a sermon than a history. The author's purpose is to teach loyalty to God's law and to praise the martyrs who died for their faith.

Second Maccabees also contains the Old Testament's only clear passage that teaches us to pray for our beloved dead because of the resurrection.

Highlights include the stirring story of the mother and seven sons who were tortured and slaughtered for their faith (chapter 7), and the teaching on the resurrection of the dead (6:26; 7:9; 12:41-46; 14:46) and on the intercessory prayers of the saints in heaven (15:12-16) where Jeremiah the prophet is seen praying in heaven for Judas Maccabeus on earth. The church militant on earth and the church triumphant in heaven are one. In prayer they have real contact with each other. Death no more destroys or even separates God's people, the church, the New Israel, than it could destroy or separate ancient Israel. "Therefore, since we are surrounded by so great a cloud of witnesses, let us also lay aside every weight and sin which clings so closely, and let us run with perseverance the race that is set before us, . . ." (Hebrews 12:1).

FIRST ESDRAS: SECOND CHRONICLES 35-36, EZRA, AND NEHEMIAH 6-8 RETOLD

The *First* and *Second Books of Esdras* and the *Prayer of Manasseh* are *not* part of the seventy-two books which the Catholic church accepts as the canon or list of books of Scripture (that is, divinely inspired, authoritative, and infallible). But they are wise and useful reading. The reason they are included as part of the Apocrypha in many Catholic and Protestant Bibles is because the Jews in Alexandria, Egypt who made the Septuagint Greek translation of the Old Testament did include them, because some Protestants (mainly Anglicans and Episcopalians) include them as part of their Apocrypha, and because they were used by Christians for the first few centuries. In fact, some Orthodox churches, which have no closed second canon of Scripture, hold that *First* and *Second Esdras* are "inspired."

The events told in the *First Book of Esdras* are also told in 2 Chronicles 35-36, *Ezra,* and Nehemiah 6-8. But *First Esdras* adds the interesting philosophical debate of the bodyguards before the emperor (chapters 3-4).

SECOND ESDRAS: APOCALYPTIC VISIONS

Most of this book consists of seven apocalyptic visions, that is, visions of the end of the world and the crises that are to come before the end. It offers answers to some of the greatest philosophical questions asked in any time: questions about the problem of evil and suffering and about the meaning and end of history. The style is more philosophical than that of the canonical books of Scripture, and more typical of the Greek mind than the Hebrew mind.

What are we to make of prophecies and visions like these that are not in the canon of Scripture but seem to be wise and edifying? On the one hand, they are not infallible. We cannot be certain that they are true. On the other hand, when they dovetail nicely with Scripture, when they explain Scripture and when Scripture explains them, we should give them a respectful hearing and get from them the wisdom and inspiration they have to offer.

THE PRAYER OF MANASSEH: A PRAYER OF REPENTANCE

The story of Manasseh, who was a very evil king of Judah, is told in 2 Chronicles 33. This short prayer is a prayer of repentance for sin. Whether Manasseh actually composed it or not, it is a beautiful prayer to use. It begins and ends with praise, which is the main theme of prayer in the Bible, and encloses repentance in that context.

What Next?

I F YOU HAVE READ THIS BOOK, you are probably a beginner in reading and studying the Bible. Certainly, no Scripture scholar should need to read a beginner's book like this one. So what's your next step?

Not more "advanced" books *about* the Bible (at least not yet), but the Bible itself.

If you were foolish enough to read this book *instead* of reading the Bible, my book instead of God's book, then now's the time to exchange that foolishness for wisdom.

If you read this book *together with* the Bible, as it is meant to be read, then now's the time to dig more deeply into the Bible, the most inexhaustible book ever written, the book that the world's greatest minds have never exhausted and the world's simplest minds have always understood, the book that infinitely rewards endless rereading. As one poet put it:

Thy Word is like a garden, Lord,
With flowers bright and fair;
And everyone who comes may pluck
A lovely cluster there.
Thy Word is like a deep, deep mine. . . .

I wish you many happy hours exploring this mine. It contains the world's most precious diamonds, formed under centuries of pressure. And it tells you above all about one "pearl of great value" (Matthew 13:46) that is worth selling everything that you have for. And best of all, that pearl is free! (See Revelations 22:17.)